INSIDE
PRIVATE EYE

INSIDE
PRIVATE EYE

Peter McKay

Fourth Estate · LONDON

First published in Great Britain in 1986 by
Fourth Estate Ltd
113 Westbourne Grove
London W2 4UP
Telephone 01 727 8993/243 1382

Copyright © Peter McKay
Illustrations by Willie Rushton

British Library Cataloguing in Publication Data

McKay, Peter
    Inside Private eye
    1. Private eye
    I. Title
    827'.914'09   PN5130.P7

ISBN 0-947795-80-4

The publishers wish to thank all those who have given permission for
copyright material to be reproduced in this book.

Typeset in Palatino by
Avocet, Greyhound House, Bicester Road, Launton, Oxfordshire OX6 0DQ.
Printed and bound by
Richard Clay (The Chaucer Press) Ltd, Bungay, Suffolk.

CONTENTS

ACKNOWLEDGEMENTS

The author wishes to thank:
Carla 'Doxy' Dobson, for the Glossary of Gnomespeak
Richard Ingrams
Patrick Marnham
Graham Bridgstock

LIST OF ILLUSTRATIONS
Between pages 96 and 97

PREFACE

In March of 1986 the editor of *Private Eye* magazine, Richard Ingrams, who was forty-eight, announced that he was standing down in favour of his twenty-four-year-old protégé, Ian Hislop. The news was put out by the Press Association and became the subject of long stories in the serious newspapers. Mr Ingrams and Mr Hislop were booked to appear on the 'Wogan' TV show.

Few resignations in Fleet Street, in broadcasting or in the magazine community could have caused so much stir. Indeed, the affair got as much, if not more, coverage than the resignation of a cabinet minister might have done.

Oddly, no one seemed to think the fuss was overdone. Nor did anyone venture to query the circumstances under which a tired editor – usually a creature most vulnerable to brutal sacking – was able to choose his successor without consulting anyone.

Private Eye is a unique and mysterious institution. It has grown from a home typed joke sheet started with £450 in 1961 into a powerful scandal magazine with more than one million readers and an annual turnover of over £3 million. From the John Profumo Affair of the 1960s to the resignation of Cecil Parkinson in the 1980s, *Private Eye* has uncovered or commented pungently on all the rows, scandals and intrigues of the past twenty-five years. Yet its workings have remained mysterious to contributors and readers

7

alike. Many who buy it do not understand half of its contents. While other magazines and newspapers strive to make things simpler for their readers, *Private Eye* behaves like a private joke club on which the public is allowed to eavesdrop – at a price of forty-five pence every fortnight. Malcolm Muggeridge's description of it in the 1960s was: 'It's like a smart country house party putting on a show for the servants.'

Who exactly is Baillie Vass, and what is his connection to Lord Home of the Hirsel? Why is 'Grovel' so called, and when Ingrams talks of his 'organ' does he mean an intensely personal protuberation, the magazine, or the ancient instrument he plays so ardently in the church near his Berkshire home?

Each fortnight, a baffling gallery of alleged crooks, conmen, idiots and clowns are produced for the delectation of *Private Eye* readers – many of them partly or even wholly concealed by arcane nicknames and appellations. Sometimes stories are completely wrong, sometimes half wrong. Others are repeated and some are very pointless and boring.

Yet readers who seethe, for instance, over Larry Adler's convoluted letters to the editor, and write in demanding that the publicity-mad mouth organist be gagged, miss the point: the letters are published *because* they annoy readers. When others write to complain of an unfunny joke going on and on they, too, miss the point: jokes, stories, cartoons – even letters from readers – are not put in for the readers' benefit; they are put in largely to amuse those who compose the magazine. *Private Eye* is the only magazine with the gall to inform subscribers: 'Long boring letters will be cut.'

Scarcely a week passes without news of *Private Eye* in the press. Usually it is the announcement of another libel action averted by retraction, a grovelling apology, and/or a promise to pay damages. It literally thrives on the condemnation of judges: libel actions, or the threat of them, have played a major part in driving its sales up to around 250,000 a fortnight by the end of 1986.

No magazine or paper in this country this century has attracted so much attention, good and bad. *Private Eye* has enemies among Tories and socialists, Arabs and Jews, men and women. Financier Sir James Goldsmith, who was reputed to have received a knighthood from the Wilson government for his attempts to silence *Private Eye*, called it the 'pus' leaking from the wounds of a sick society. And, after a quarter of a century, the late writer Kenneth Tynan's rhetorical question – 'When are you going to get a point of view?' – remains unanswered.

But if you have a story that might bring down the government, disgrace the Royal Family, or cause pandemonium in the streets, *Private Eye* remains your best chance of exposing it to the light of day. The magazine employs no full-time journalists, yet it lands some of the biggest stories of the day through a labyrinth of Fleet Street, Westminster and City conduits. It is the beneficiary of Goldsmith's despised 'see-through society' in which information is used, or misused, in the daily struggle for individual, corporate and political power. One of its most bitter enemies, the journalist and litigant Nora Beloff, was once obliged to admit: '*Private Eye* does mix up its filth with genuine revelations.'

It is not read in every household, but it has become a household name – the subject of hundreds of long newspaper and magazine articles and TV documentaries. Its mockeries and its jokes seem to percolate through the national consciousness. During the 1970 general election, Prime Minister Edward Heath was heckled by schoolchildren calling out his *Eye* nickname – 'Gro-cer, Gro-cer'. They had no idea where the name had come from.

People are fascinated, as well as repelled, by its power and its recklessness. Writers who praised it to the heavens in the early days now fear and hate it. The editors of newspapers which outsell it twenty times over fear being mentioned in its 'Street of Shame' column. MPs on the crest of promotion become heartsick at the prospect of attracting the baleful attention of its 'Backbiter' column. Business tycoons, whose nightmare is an appearance in the 'In the

City' column, send researchers to *Private Eye* to look through back issues for damaging material with which to attack rivals. Socialites pass compromising information about rivals to 'Grovel' in exchange for discretion on the subject of their own lives.

Private Eye excoriates capitalism, yet it is a shining example of successful private enterprise. Every scrap of its material is used and re-used; every modest comic device, once tested in its pages, is launched with others in book form. Successful jokes such as 'Mrs Wilson's Diary' and 'Dear Bill' are marketed separately and successfully. Their humour has been bowdlerised in a James Bond film, adapted to the West End stage, transcribed onto long-playing records and injected into TV shows from 'That Was The Week That Was' in the 1960s to 'Spitting Image' in the 1980s. But although the magazine had made millions, its shareholders have never received a penny of dividend.

Towards the end of 1986, and its twenty-fifth anniversary, great changes took place. Ingrams' announced retirement created a struggle for power. New feuds began among the satirists and old ones were revived. There was a possibility that the whole pack of cards would collapse.

I was drawn into *Private Eye* in 1972 by Patrick Marnham, then the author of the 'Grovel' column and later of *The Private Eye Story*. I have contributed to every section of the magazine – writing stories, selecting items for 'Pseuds' Corner, and 'I Spy', as well as dreaming up, with Richard Ingrams, the 'Sir Jonah Junor' column.

When I told an otherwise on-the-ball *Eye* subscriber and friend recently about this collaboration, he looked puzzled, and finally said he had always believed it was written by the *Sunday Express*'s then editor, Sir John Junor – the man the 'Sir Jonah' column was intended to satirize. We agreed that the Eye was full of such misunderstandings, and he said: 'You should write a book about it.'

Here it is.

Chapter One

Private Eye As We Know It

Sitting behind a plain, battered old desk piled high with newspaper clippings, anonymous poison pen letters and suggestions for jokes, Richard Reid Ingrams might easily be taken for the headmaster of a minor public school who cherishes his reputation for eccentricity. Around him are several photographs of eminent people he has not met, but who have entered his private demonology. A life-size cardboard cut-out photograph of one, the financier Sir James Goldsmith, watches from the corner, a cheery, hesitant smile – the smile of a man facing newspaper flashguns – frozen on his full, not to say fat, features. First-time visitors to the Ingrams sanctum sometimes jump with fright when they catch sight of it out of the corner of their eye.

Ingrams was born in August 1937. He is six feet and two inches tall, and his face is pockmarked with the campaign scars of adolescent acne wars. His brown hair is now pepper and salted; his eyes are pale blue. Lady profile writers who have ascended these stairs with spiral notebooks have judged him to be craggily handsome. 'It's difficult to explain how wonderful he is,' sighed one old friend, Candida Lycett Green, 'but he exudes goodness and a faint holiness.' Her late father, Poet Laureate Sir John Betjeman, might have chosen instead to compare Ingrams to an early Anglo-Saxon place of worship.

For years there has been a studied casualness in his clothes. He has always favoured sturdy corduroy jackets,

11

but not of the type available in Harrods or other expensive outfitters. His plain woollen sweaters generally have holes at the armpit and dribble aimlessly over his shirt cuffs onto his wrists. In central Soho, the habitat of film industry types in sleek dark cloth bedecked with the accessories of youthful high fashion, he cuts an unusual figure as he strides along in his large, brown working shoes. He takes no great trouble with his hair, which he has cut in a short-back-and-sides fashion at a local barber when its length starts to become noticeable. His teeth are quite badly stained, although much improved since he discovered the wonderful effects of using wooden toothpicks after lunch.

He gives the overall impression of a man whose relaxed physical habits are frozen in his late teens, and who at the same time relishes the sanctuary of middle age. This can make some elements of his character seem contradictory. He has the flashing, slightly cruel wit and sudden bright smile of a young man together with a fondness for adopting old fogey, *grand seigneur* roles in conversation. For years he had kept a selection of walking sticks at his home.

It was at Shrewsbury school that, in 1952, he met Paul Foot, William Rushton and Christopher Booker. They became friends for life, as well as joint editors of a school magazine, *The Salopian*. After Oxford, Foot went off to Glasgow to sharpen his socialist wits and hone his journalistic talents on the lively pages of the tabloid *Daily Record*. After losing £3,000 of his own money trying to become a theatrical impresario, Ingrams joined up with Rushton and Booker, who had started *Private Eye* magazine in 1961. A review of this enterprise in the *Observer* at the time included brief portraits of the trio that are still recognisable twenty-five years later.

Ingrams, 'a big fellow with a caveman look'; Booker, 'bespectacled with bantering talk and a mauve striped shirt'; Rushton, 'rotund and quizzical'. The brilliant photographer Jane Bown took a picture of them on a staircase with Nicholas Luard, a dapper Old Etonian who was the magazine's business manager, sitting at their feet. Their relationship with business advisors was to remain ducal.

There were early struggles for control which resulted in Ingrams devoting his life to the magazine while Booker and Rushton became satirical satellites. This was not accomplished without blood on the floor, but the depth of their early regard for one another carried all of them through together to the calmer waters of mellow friendship in middle age. Booker, Rushton and Foot have all become famous outside *Private Eye*, but Ingrams has identified himself so closely with it that his fame is inextricably bound up with that of his magazine. His friends can only accommodate his eminence by giving him the honorary title of Lord Gnome.

At *Private Eye* we have amused ourselves for years by submitting elements of his character to amateur, *Reader's Digest*-type psychological analyses. The findings have included the theory that his outward appearance and remote, enigmatic manner are designed to discourage the advances of women. Some say the reverse is true, suggesting that his schoolboy appearance means he seeks the protection as well as the love of women.

Up to the age of thirty he smoked cigarettes, drank wine, whisky, beer and brandy, and enjoyed doing the rounds of Soho nightclubs. Then in 1967 he abandoned those pleasures. He said he had received medical advice to the effect that he would die if he continued to drink. Drinking friends, including Auberon Waugh, Richard West and Jeffrey Bernard – the latter recognised as an outstanding expert in this field – have always cast doubt on this story. There was speculation instead of some 'Road to Damascus' moral reason for the sudden withdrawal.

Ingrams himself is content to stick to his story, elaborating it only with a quote from Dr Johnson: 'Abstinence is as easy to me as temperance would be difficult.' Yet Ingrams likes to socialise with drinkers, his frequent lunchtime rendezvous being the Coach and Horses pub at the corner of Greek and Romilly Streets, Soho.

There he sips mineral water; but is not reluctant to fetch and pay for the alcoholic drinks preferred by his friends and colleagues. Enemies describe him as a 'reformed alcoholic'. He is often visited at the pub by his children – Fred, an aspiring artist employed by *Punch* magazine, and Margaret ('Jubby'), who works for the Palestinian publisher Naim Attallah. Both son and daughter like to drink, and their father gives no sign that he disapproves unduly.

He says of his son: 'I don't on the whole want to mould Fred. I never have. I did offer him a hundred quid if he didn't smoke by the age of twenty-one, and that was lost early on.'

Fred says of his father: 'When I was little I used to be quite frightened of him. I would never have been disrespectful. He was very quiet. His only guidance would be on what books I should read, what paintings I should look at, and telling me what I shouldn't be looking at, like the television. He never shouted at me or raised his voice towards me or my sister. He was just very quiet, just a presence.'

Ingrams stoops slightly, and walks with a swift, almost scurrying gait. He inclines his head to the left while walking, and carries his papers in a cheap, imitation leather travel bag. In middle age he has developed a slight pre-occupation with madness, thinking some of his friends have become 'loopy'.

Sharing an office with Ingrams is Ian Hislop, born a year before *Private Eye* was founded. After five years of contributing jokes he became editor-designate, as well as principal writer on the Central TV satirical puppet show, 'Spitting Image'.

Hislop is, in Lord Beaverbrook's self-serving usage, 'small in stature'. His detractors like to undermine his claims to boyish youthfulness by pointing out that he is balding. He is a tiny, tubby man in baggy, nondescript clothes, although he does sometimes make a dashing effort by wearing a narrow leather tie.

While at Oxford he interviewed Ingrams for the undergraduate lampoon *Passing Wind*. Both found the experience a rewarding one, and Ian was later to submit joke ideas to *Private Eye*. The best remembered one was a send-up of the *Observer* colour magazine 'A Room Of My Own' series. Each week an eminent person would be photographed in their favourite room, discussing their possessions. Hislop devised a skit and cartoon of the IRA hunger striker Bobby Sands in his excrement-coated cell.

Hislop is usually cheerful. But the resistance of *Eye* colleagues to his gradual assumption of editorial responsibilities has caused him often to exhibit a hectoring, slightly bullying manner, which is much resented, particularly among the women.

Above and below Ingrams and Hislop in the splendid, listed Soho leasehold building, *Eye* employees work on stories, jokes, cartoons and accounts. The atmosphere is that of a low-key advertising agency, or perhaps a middle-ranking charity.

In the comfortable ground-floor room overlooking Carlisle Street sit Hilary Lowinger, forty-one, and Maggie Lunn, twenty-five, who attend to the switchboard and the reception. Hilary is a bubbly married lady. Maggie is a perky single girl and an exile from the north-east of England. There's a shabby old sofa for those who wait there and fresh coffee brewing at most times. Guests may be offered a biscuit.

To the rear of the ground floor Tony Rushton, a thin, unsmiling man of forty-five, works at his draughtsman's board. Deceptively mild in manner, he conducts advertising work and layout design with a repressed air of tension that occasionally explodes into rage when he is thwarted or has his space invaded. He is a cousin of Willie Rushton, and he also went to Shrewsbury. But he does not enjoy a close rapport with Ingrams, who delights in upsetting him. When he occupied an office directly below Ingrams at the old Greek Street premises, the editor would torment Rushton by drumming his heels on the floor every time the designer coughed or sneezed. Rushton was in at the beginning, co-opted into satire by his cousin while at a loose end in the 1960s. Ingrams enjoys unsettling 'Tone' by setting him difficult tasks, and from time to time chopping and changing his job.

Like Ingrams, Rushton completed National Service. He entered the Royal Marines while Ingrams became a sergeant in the Royal Army Educational Corps. Rushton likes to speculate about his editor's attitudes. He thinks Ingrams' famous distaste for 'homosexualists' might easily be the result of an assault during his army days. Ingrams retorts that Rushton might be attributing to him a dark experience of his own.

At another desk sits tall, blonde Elizabeth Elliott, who is forty-one. She graduated from the front office to write the 'Sally Deedes' consumer complaints column. She once enjoyed a warm, almost flirtatious relationship with Ingrams, but his attitude to her changed after she became a companion of a *Sunday Times* journalist, Henry Porter, whom Ingrams said he disliked and distrusted, and by whom she had a baby.

Cyril Bottomley, a white-haired former newsprint salesman who now buys paper for *Private Eye* – thus cutting out the middlemen for whom he once used to toil – sometimes occupies a desk there, too. He is a lifelong *Daily Express* reader, and is cosily known as Mr B.

In the office next to Ingrams on the first floor is New Zealander Paul Halloran, an *Eye* reporter who augments his earnings by tipping off several Fleet Street papers. He is also the principal conduit of *Private Eye* news to Fleet Street, as well as an adroit broadcaster of disinformation when Ingrams thinks such a course is necessary. Halloran's contributions are intended for the back of the magazine. He is not a natural writer by any means, and turning his complex sentences into understandable journalism imposes a great, if lightly borne, burden on the Australian sub-editor Mary Brooks, who left in 1986.

Portly in build, with an aggressive, irascible manner, Halloran is given to conspiratorial activities – a legacy, say some, of an earlier life as a New Zealand labour relations official. His telephone is fixed to tape record telephone conversations, and colleagues speculate darkly about the purpose of his frequent foreign travels, which are neither financed by nor connected to his *Eye* activities.

Halloran cultivates his image as *Private Eye*'s mystery man by staying away from occasions at which photographers are expected, as Greta Garbo used to do. He missed the black tie ball held at the Reform Club to celebrate *Private Eye*'s twenty-first anniversary, but decided instead to arrange for bogus invitations to be sent to prominent people who were *Eye* figures of fun. Edward Heath was one, Tory MP Teddy Taylor another. Heath replied frostily that he would be unable to come, but Taylor accepted. It then had to be broken to him, in a letter from Ingrams, that the invitation was bogus, and Taylor wrote a bitter letter of regret in reply.

Halloran is often very rude to visitors to *Private Eye*, as well as to guests at the fortnightly luncheons. But Ingrams tolerates his brusque ways. Resentful colleagues say Halloran is Ingrams' watchdog, and the master is never better pleased than when he sees his florid-faced charge in hot pursuit of an irritant.

On the third floor is Christopher Silvester, aged twenty-five, who is also an *Eye* reporter. Unlike the casual Halloran, who often favours lively Hawaiian shirts and white shoes, Silvester is something of a dandy. He is perhaps the only reporter in London who still wears spats. He specialises in composing disrespectful political notes for the 'Backbiter' column, designed to ridicule or reduce in public esteem those politicians who do not meet his own high standard of excellence and probity. In contrast with Halloran, Silvester shows all the nimble sure-footedness in his journalism that his grandfather, the late band leader Victor Silvester, displayed on the dance floor. But his work poses problems for the lawyer who comes in on each publishing Monday to undertake the Herculean and rather comical task of reading *Private Eye* for libels. Silvester's ambition is to be a Conservative MP, and he has the encouraging incentive of knowing that his predecessor as 'Backbiter', Keith Raffan, landed a then safe Welsh constituency.

Silvester's office was once the roost of Auberon Waugh, and a stuffed dog used by the great Somerset man of letters for photographic purposes – the cover of a book – still sits patiently on the shelves, forlornly awaiting the call of his master, the literary squire of Combe Florey.

Ingrams is fond of Silvester, who once courted his daughter Margaret. He managed the delicate task of extricating himself from the relationship without being horse-whipped – or sacked. Ingrams sees in Silvester a perverse quality he noted years ago in an Oxford friend, Noel Picarda. Silvester is a man of a myriad schemes, but few of them have yet become successful. To Ingrams, Silvester's lack of success is 'his saving grace'.

Sheila Molnar, a gentle Welsh-born young married woman of thirty-six who is the magazine's company secretary and accountant, occupies the office next door. She takes photographs at many of the *Eye* functions, and operates a coffee pot for those unwilling to descend to the front office.

On the fourth floor sits David Cash, *Private Eye*'s managing director and a part-time East Sussex farmer. His shelves overflow with *Eye* books, and his walls are adorned with circulation charts that attest to the magazine's growing popularity. Cash is also small in stature, a shortcoming he alleviates partially by his habit of walking on the tips of his toes. He was also once rotund in build, before he discovered the wonders of London exercise studios and diets.

Over the years *Private Eye* has also employed or been assisted by a number of MPs, starting with the late Labour member Tom Driberg. Driberg set an obscene crossword for the *Eye* which was popular among a wide cross-section of readers: Rosalind Runcie, whose husband, the Bishop of St Albans, was to rise even higher in the Church of England, admits to being an early devotee of the Driberg fortnightly poser.

Driberg was a homosexual, and at the *Eye* he nursed an

unrequited passion for at least two colleagues: Steve Mann, a slight, dark-haired young man who then operated the typesetting machine, and Patrick Marnham, who gave up training to be a barrister for the more certain employment of conducting the 'Grovel' column. Driberg sat by as Mann typeset the crossword, and when his sheep-eyed gaze elicited no encouragement he would sigh: 'Oh, Steve!'

Ingrams was fond of Driberg stories, in particular the one in which the MP seduced a sturdy, kilted Scottish soldier in Edinburgh. When their passion was spent, Driberg enquired as to why his companion had become a homosexual and received the reply: 'Only sissies sleep with women.'

The main feature on the *Eye*'s back pages is 'In the City', by Slicker. Slicker is Michael Gillard, a brilliant former Fleet Street financial journalist who is now employed by Granada TV to dig out material for their documentary programme 'World in Action'. He is a darting, shadowy figure, rarely seen in the *Eye* offices. When we were casting 'The Muppets' at *Private Eye* – the staff are fond of assigning each other roles in whatever show or soap opera is popular at the time – there was not the slightest doubt about Michael's position in Ingrams' favourite TV entertainment: he was Zoot the saxophonist.

'Nooks and Corners' is written by Gavin Stamp under the pseudonym 'Piloti'. He is a young fogey who has cultivated an interest in the late architectural expert Edward James, inspiring Viscount Lambton to remark waspishly: 'Odd, aren't they, these young men who attach themselves to dead men?'

'The World of Books' is compiled with the help of several book-trade hacks, not all of whom disclose the origin of their animus against particular publishers. Geoffrey Wheatcroft of the *Standard*'s 'Londoner's Diary' was an early contibutor, until he found his feet in more orthodox journalism, as was A. N. Wilson.

The longer review is farmed out to the anonymous contributor who can best arrange a demolition job on the work in question, usually because they know something about the subject and have reason to despise the new author involved. The first-class *Eye* attack in 1986 on *The Windsor Letters*, edited by Michael Bloch, was composed in sunny Minorca by author Michael Thornton, whose own researches into the Windsor story were once impeded by Bloch and his elderly patron, Maître Suzanne Blum, the Windsors' Paris attorney.

'Pseud's Corner', once my own bailiwick, is the preserve of author and poet Christopher Logue, who also assembles the 'True Stories' from scores of readers' contributions. When Logue complained that he needed more money from the *Eye*, Ingrams increased his stipend by adding 'Pseud's Corner' to his fortnightly responsibilities. Another poet who frequents the *Eye* is Michael Horowitz, who toils for hours reproducing his poetry on the office copying machines.

'Down on the Farm', by 'Old Muckspreader', was once the work of Tory MP Sir Richard Body – he was identified during the course of an *Eye* libel case. But farmers, at which the column is primarily aimed, might have been able to identify him sooner when the diarist of *The Field* magazine remarked, apropos of nothing, that 'Old Muckspreader' would be pleased to hear of Body's knighthood. Recently, however, Body has hopped over the fence and become Chairman of the Commons Select Committee on Agriculture – a body which 'Old Muckspreader' might previously have regarded with some disgust. The column is now composed by two anonymous contributors.

This is Mockery Towers, the headquarters of Britain's satire industry. Here, an industry run on cottage craft lines supplies more than a million customers with an inimitable fortnightly portrait of the news and personalities of the day. Telephones ring; messengers arrive with advertisements and editorial matter; artists offer cartoons; journalists come to gossip. Ingrams likes to adopt the rasping Canadian drawl of the late Lord Beaverbrook to sum up his satisfaction about this odd little goldmine: 'Somethin' from nuthin', Mr McKay – what dya think a' that?'.

Until he handed over the reins of power to Ian Hislop, Ingrams worked one week on and one week off, as well as coming in on the Monday of the off week, which is publishing day. He spends his mornings dealing with stories, letters and meetings. The afternoons are for jokes. The door to Ingrams' office, usually open, is closed. A group of two or three men gather, and the editor selects a ballpoint pen and a sheet of yellow foolscap paper.

Soon, cries of laughter can be heard. A joke session is in progress. Even as he approaches the age of fifty, Ingrams is still capable of giggling until the tears run down his cheeks. He flings himself about, like a car passenger caught in a whiplash road accident, and buries his face in his hands. Some of the cries of laughter – notably those of Barry Fantoni – seem over-enthusiastic, as a contributor cheers on his idea for a skit. Occasionally Christopher Booker, known as The Deacon because of his ecclesiastical appearance as well as his philosophical skills, descends in shirtsleeves from the flaying chamber for refreshment.

Peter Cook, the majority shareholder, arrives from time to time with a joke suggested by some risible item in the tabloid newspapers. On the 'on' Monday, John Wells arrives to compose 'Dear Bill' with Ingrams. Cartoonist Michael Heath sits in Ingrams' office drawing his 'great bore' for the new issue.

On Tuesday of the on week he calls a 'hacks' meeting' at noon. Halloran, Silvester, Jane Ellison and myself are asked how we propose to fill the front section and the back pages. There is also a need to produce a 'letter from', the *Eye*'s gesture to foreign coverage. As often as not this is written in London, but it is composed in such a way – 'here in Abu Dhabi' – as to suggest it has been cabled urgently from abroad.

On working days Ingrams starts at eight in the morning to catch a train from Goring & Streatley, Oxfordshire, to Paddington. He reads the *Daily Mail* and the *Daily Telegraph*, but gave up the *Mail* in 1986 in favour of Eddy Shah's colour paper, *Today*. He professes a high regard for Mr

Shah, and an intermediary, *Today*'s managing editor at the time, Jeremy Deedes, who was a friend of Ingrams, sought to bring Shah to one of the fortnightly *Eye* lunches. But when Shah heard he was expected he cried off, saying he would only have gone if he could have turned up unexpectedly.

Ingrams holds special lunches at the Gay Hussar, where he has become a friend of the proprietor, Victor Sassie. Thinking one day that Sassie bore a resemblance to Strauss, Ingrams later accorded the restaurateur the privilege of an appearance in the *Eye*'s 'Lookalike' feature, where a fictitious reader – often 'Ena Maxwell' – draws attention to likenesses among public men (for some reason seldom women). The photo captions are always put under the wrong picture to heighten the underlying joke, which pairs up unlikely people and asks 'Are they by any chance related?'.

Each Wednesday of the on week *Private Eye* holds a lunch upstairs at the Coach and Horses, prepared by the pub's African cook Alaki and served by the sweet-natured Irish barman Michael. Alaki is fiercely protective of Ingrams, and glares at journalists who have criticised her hero in print.

Norman Balon, the landlord of the Coach and Horses, runs his pub like a martinet, shouting furiously at staff and customers alike. He once told the Labour MP Willie Hamilton to 'fuck off' because Hamilton, trying to find his way to the lunch, had the temerity to interrupt Norman while he was on the telephone. He has been compared to the American actor Walter Matthau in appearance, and indeed he is fond of the theatrical world, having become something of a fixture at first nights. Danny La Rue, John Hurt and Tom Baker are all regulars at the pub.

The table closest to the lavatories is reserved every day for the staff of *Private Eye*, but it is necessary to walk behind the bar and up the stairs to get to the private room. No one is told this, and many guests already nervous at the thought of entering such a thieves' kitchen of gossips and satirists arrive in a state of high excitement.

The *Sunday Times* commentator Peter Jenkins once arrived breathless and red in the face, shouting at Ingrams: 'Do you know what that man said to me? He told me to fuck off.' Ingrams is fond of Norman, who has often bolstered Ingrams' natural xenophobia by returning from foreign parts and saying they were terrible. When Norman returned from his first visit to New York, Ingrams, who has never been to America, was anxious for his impressions of the New World.

'I couldn't live there' said Norman of Manhattan. 'They don't have no fucking gardens.'

Ingrams repeated Norman's assessment to friends for weeks.

Ingrams likes also to attend the monthly Foyles literary lunch at the Dorchester Hotel, where – knowing his appeal to the autograph-collecting old ladies who dominate this affair – Christina Foyle seats him at the top table. There is usually a party of reporters from the gossip columns seated close to the eminent guests, who dutifully applaud as each top-table star is announced. Ingrams delights in their reaction when his turn comes: 'The hacks always hiss at me.'

If during the week he has lunched casually with the staff at the pub, he likes afterwards to roam the bookshops around Charing Cross Road, and he is known to some of their proprietors. Mary Ingrams runs a bookshop in Wallingford, Berkshire.

Another favourite pastime is to wander into shops selling stationery. I too have this weakness, and we have agreed that a growing preoccupation with new stationery products and gadgets may be a sign of madness.

Ingrams also likes to visit the pub for an hour after work, taking great delight in observing the denizens of what he calls 'Winos' Corner' – a coterie of hard-drinking journalists and actors who, having conversed at a reasonable level at lunchtime, by evening are usually shouting at the tops of their voices. Sometimes, when the din and rows get out of hand, Ingrams will shout, 'Norman!' – upon which the custodian of the Coach appears, cursing the miscreants and bravely restoring order with no thought to his own safety.

After his refreshing glass or two of Perrier, Ingrams walks to the Underground. He occasionally takes a cab and hates it when cabbies recognise him, for they are often tempted to sound off about the latest issues of the day. Ingrams has waged a valuable campaign against loquacious cabmen in the *Eye* in the form of a column in which a fictitious driver – usually with a Jewish-sounding name – rants on about stringing people up.

On the train home from Paddington he occasionally arranges earphones on his head and listens to classical music on a Sony Walkman. He excuses this lapse into the world of modern contrivances by saying it repels bores. Ingrams would have justified the Second World War by saying it repelled bores.

By 1986, Ingrams is well off, if not rich. There is no mortgage on the beautiful old converted forge in Aldworth, Berkshire, which is worth about £150,000, and he has purchased a beach bungalow in Rye, close to the Romney Marshes, by which he is fascinated. Both he and his wife Mary have inherited money, and his total earnings are close to £40,000 a year.

Mary's Irish family is moderately well off, and Ingrams' grandmother was a member of the Baring banking family. His grandfather was Sir James Reid, an Aberdeen doctor who served Queen Victoria. Ingrams spent his earliest years at his mother's family home at Ellon, Aberdeenshire, where he attended the local state school.

Ingrams hardly knew his father, Leonard St Clair Ingrams, an investment banker who died of a heart attack in his early fifties when Richard was fifteen. But it was sometimes said that their careers had one amusing similarity. During the war Leonard Ingrams worked on anti-Nazi propaganda, which included dropping leaflets full of misleading information designed to undermine those in power. Many believe that *Private Eye* serves the same purpose in post-War Britain.

Leonard Ingrams had been a friend of the French playwright Jean Cocteau, who was a homosexual. A guest to Aldworth once found a volume by Cocteau in the book-lined bedroom to which he had been assigned for the night. Inside it was a letter to Richard Ingrams from the late literary critic Cyril Connolly concerning Leonard Ingrams' relationship with Cocteau. Connolly had known both men and it was evident that Ingrams had asked him about their friendship. He discovered that his father was a heroic character in one of Cocteau's books.

Ingrams' view of homosexuality is that it is avoidable, rather like heterosexual promiscuity. His view of homosexuality carries the implication that many men have homosexual tendencies but repress them – which coincides with the argument of those he most opposes, homosexual proselytizers.

During the Jeremy Thorpe case he was most impressed by an article written by Auberon Waugh, who largely shares his views on homosexuality, saying that gays suppressed one rather obvious drawback of their habit – that buggery was a painful act.

But Ingrams has never to my knowledge discriminated against homosexuals in public or private life. Like Beaverbrook with Tom Driberg, he regretted their homosexuality, but separated the man from the habit.

Ingrams admires greatly his maternal grandfather, Sir James Reid, especially for the Aberdeen physician's dry wit. He likes one story about a dinner at Balmoral attended by his grandfather, at which, unusually for Queen Victoria, wine was served. The butler explained that they might toast the Queen's dear, departed Prince Consort Albert, whose birthday fell on that day. Sir James considered this touching proposition and replied: 'I have no objection.'

On another occasion Sir James was asked for his advice on the position of an Indian who had assumed a large role in the lonely old sovereign's life. This man was something of a fraud, but he was persuasive and he had Victoria's attention. She wanted to allow him to travel with her to Paris and objections had been aired by several courtiers. The wise

Aberdonian doctor was asked by Victoria for his opinion, and he unhesitatingly came out against the idea. 'The people will laugh at you, Ma'am,' he said, with brutal honesty.

Mary Ingrams is a large-boned, handsome Irishwoman, fond of horses and country life. She has a brusque manner, and does not care to be overly nice to those whom she does not respect. She likes to drink and smoke, and calls Ingrams 'Ditch' (Paul Foot is the only other Ingrams intimate I have ever heard use that name for him). Fond of gossip, Mary would often fill me in on Berkshire society affairs when I wrote the William Hickey column in the *Daily Express*.

It was the normal practice to send a small cheque to the mischievious souls who risked the wrath of their important friends by assisting gossip columnists. But Mary was always careful to refuse payment unless it was sent to a charity. She did say she would accept an item from the shop Hermes from time to time, but there were always practical difficulties in making such an arrangement. In the seventies Richard and Mary parted for two months, Richard staying with the Foots in London. Much was made of the idea that *Private Eye*'s hold on the Fleet Street gossip columnists was such that the story never appeared. But the reason it never appeared was that the gossip columnists involved – Nigel Dempster and myself – did not know about it. And by the time we heard, at least a year later, the Ingramses had long been back together again. Even the most skilled gossip columnist would have difficulty in making such an item interesting. But those who enjoyed conspiracy theories – usually journalists who had been attacked in *Private Eye* for far more entertaining and newsworthy misdemeanours – would fulminate against this shocking abuse of the public's right to know.

The marriage of one prominent newspaper executive, by contrast, had disintegrated in far more newsworthy circumstances that were duly reported in the *Eye*. He had taken his mistress, who was to become his third wife, to Wimbledon, and they were seated in close proximity to the scoreboard.

Each time the camera swung away from the action and zoomed in to pick up the score, there was the beaming newspaper man with the new love of his life, who was also fortunate enough to be his secretary. When the happy pair returned to the office together, the man's wife was waiting for them. She had been observing the proceedings on the TV at home.

Ingrams and Mary have had three children, but the youngest boy, Arthur, died. He was severely handicapped and was never able to walk. He is now buried in the church-yard close to the Ingrams' home. A reference to Arthur by Christopher Silvester in a 1986 *Listener* profile of Ingrams was considered tasteless by Fred Ingrams.

> I have known Richard, inasmuch as anyone can know that Sphinx-like person, from both sides. I have caught him weeping in the flickering half light of an Oxford cinema at the scene in Laurence Olivier's Hamlet when that troubled prince is told of Ophelia's suicide. I have seen him tearful at a concert performed of Elgar's First Symphony. I have stood in silence with him at the grave of his son Arthur in Aldworth churchyard. I have walked with him on the Berkshire downs and heard him bitterly lament the bygone age of mixed farming before the English countryside was raped by plough and combine harvester.

Richard Ingrams sent a copy of the piece back to Silvester with a kindly note on top saying: '3/10 – shows promise. RI.'

Mary Ingrams rarely visits *Private Eye*, although she helped to sell it in its earliest days. But she entertains the staff once a year when a cricket team composed of *Eye* friends and contributors plays against a local side. These are slightly awkward affairs, during which private friends of the Ingrams are exposed to *Eye* colleagues they might not otherwise have been keen to meet.

I recall one occasion when Peter Jay, who was still bathed in the glory of having been 'Our Man in Washington', split his cricket flannels in front of Nigel Dempster, who could

27

hardly be blamed for recording this significant diplomatic rupture in his column two days later. Dempster also claimed that the plump daughter of another guest, Irishman Henry Kelly, a budding television star, over-compensated for past Irish suffering by eating a whole bowl of potatoes.

In the days prior to the big row over Cecil Parkinson, Dempster and I frequently enjoyed lunch with Ingrams at the Gay Hussar. Sometimes Paul Foot would come along, and at other times the Greek gossip writer Taki Theadora-copoulos would be there. Taki told outrageous stories about society figures, but as a friend of both Sir James Goldsmith and John Aspinall, both bitter enemies of *Private Eye*, he was careful not to mention anything that was too much to their discredit.

He would always insist on paying for the lunch; Dempster is likewise most unhappy if he cannot pay for lunch. It was necessary to arrange with the restaurant staff in advance if you wanted to prevent either from doing so. Our table would be a noisy one. Dempster is more of an anecdotalist than a conversationalist – he likes to tell absurdly exaggerated stories in which he acts the parts of the protagonists.

One he was most fond of involved a duke who threw a Stilton cheese onto the table of a party of Americans. This, according to Dempster, caused carnage, and the American host demanded to see the manager. When this figure arrived he told the Americans: 'There's nothing to be done. His Grace is allowed to throw cheese.' Ingrams always roared at the story, although he would say afterwards that he did not believe it.

Another favourite Dempster anecdote concerned the newspaper editor Charles Wintour, whose daughter Anna he had once courted. Wintour did not think much of the match and, according to Dempster, spied on them. Wintour is an austere socialist who wears Hush Puppies, while Dempster is a sleekly-tailored figure in Gucci loafers. Dempster, by his own account, was dallying on the

Wintour sofa one evening with the attractive Anna, when a sudden movement caused him to glance up and behold an appalling sight: the (occupied) Hush Puppies of Charles Wintour projecting out from under a curtain.

Ingrams is not a snob and has always been happy to draw his friends from a wide social group. And although he often complains of tiredness, many consider his life an ideal one. He has his part-time job editing *Private Eye*, which he described in his *Who's Who* entry as a hobby. There are the radio and TV programmes on which he appears – he is loath to turn down any such opportunities. He contributed articles on TV to *The Spectator* for a time, and he has written books for fun rather than for money.

He has seen his friends, contemporaries – and enemies – rise to great heights, and then fall out of favour. He was highly critical of Peter Jay for seeking the glory of the Washington Embassy and, although he was fond of Jay, part of him relished the ex-envoy's gradual decline when his term was complete.

It was the same with Paul Foot, who joined, left, joined and again left *Private Eye*, before settling as campaigning journalist in residence at Robert Maxwell's *Daily Mirror*. Ingrams considers Foot to be a brilliant man destroyed by politics.

When I was sent to Washington by the *Daily Mail*, Ingrams said it was a bad move – nothing good could come of it; there was no point in living among Americans; and Fleet Street would soon forget that I existed. John Junor took the same line.

But whatever else happened in the world, Richard Ingrams would always be there, editing *Private Eye*, popping up on telly and radio, rumbling around bookshops and working on his long-term project – the official biography of his idol, Malcolm Muggeridge. Then one day he told us he was going to stand down.

Chapter Two

The End of *Private Eye* (As We Know It)

When the staff of *Private Eye* assembled at l'Escargot restaurant in Soho on Friday 14 March 1986, there was happy
anticipation of an entertaining lunch. But for some of them
it would all end in tears as realisation dawned that, to quote
the *Eye*'s legendary correspondent Lunchtime O'Booze,
'nushin' would ever be the shame again'.

Ostensibly the occasion was held to honour the departure
from the *Eye* after sixteen years of the man many would
argue was its most consistently brilliant and effective contributor, Auberon Waugh. He had accepted an offer to
become editor of the *Literary Review*, a part-time £17,000-a-
year post.

Although Waugh was to continue his journalism in the
Daily Mail, Sunday Telegraph, the *Spectator* and *Harpers and
Queen* – as well as accept one-off assignments from else-
where – he had decided to give up *Private Eye*.

Waugh was for years one of the few *Eye* contributors
permitted to have his own by-line (another was Penny
Junor). His column was a provocative amalgam of fact and
fantasy, composed in the form of diary. Few public figures
who were not his personal friends could long escape
ridicule there.

His relationship with Ingrams had always been cautiously
cordial. The editor reserved the right to review the Waugh
column before the magazine went to press, but only on a
very few occasions did he strike out an offending word or

sentence. Hislop took on this delicate role during Ingrams'
rare absences, and had recently incurred Waugh's wrath by
excising a reference to Barry Fantoni, an *Eye* contributor
from the earliest days.

Waugh's principal weapon has always been irony – so
heavy in some cases that both the victims and the readership might be forgiven for taking his column at face value.
On this occasion he recalls saying of Fantoni, whom he
liked to ridicule, 'something to the effect of how handsome
and witty he was . . .' Hislop struck it out.

This has been offered by some as one of the reasons
Waugh finally decided to go. Another is that Ingrams had,
while Waugh was on holiday, inserted a line at the foot of
the page usually occupied by his diary saying 'Auberon
Waugh has been sacked' – supposedly because Waugh had
been rude in print elsewhere about Mary Ingrams' bookshop in Wallingford.

In reality, Waugh is fond of Ingrams, and he says he just
got tired of writing the fortnightly diary. After sixteen years
he felt that he was beginning to repeat himself, and that he
needed a change. As the son of Evelyn Waugh, and the
grandson of a publisher, the *Literary Review* job was attractive because it gave him an opportunity to strike back at the
poseurs who he feels have hijacked the world of letters. The
l'Escargot luncheon, at which Waugh was to be presented
with a silver-plated wine funnel, had been postponed for
two weeks, after his sister Margaret was killed in a London
street accident. Ingrams attended the funeral.

'Bron' sat next to Ingrams at the long table overlooking
Dean Street. Others present were Willie Rushton,
Christopher Silvester, Tony Rushton, Dave Cash, Elizabeth
Elliott, Jane Ellison, Sheila Molnar, Mary Brooks, Hilary,
Maggie and myself. Hislop arrived just after the lunch had
started and, from the three empty seats available, took the
one next to Ingrams – a move that did not escape teasing
comment about his 'sitting next to teacher'.

Ingrams gave a gently witty speech about Bron's contribution to the *Eye* – laughingly quoting readers who said his

departure was a good thing. Then he took everyone by surprise by saying he, too, had an announcement to make. In September he would step down as editor and hand over to Ian.

There was a shocked silence, broken by Willie Rushton who said, 'About time too!', before striding out of the room. Elizabeth Elliott and Sheila Molnar burst into tears, and there was a growing chorus of disbelief. Silvester lightened the increasingly heavy atmosphere by jumping up, thrusting out his hand and saying to Hislop: 'Let me be the first to toady to you.'

Waugh rose to speak. He affected not to know Hislop's name, a favourite Waugh method of putting down those of whom he disapproves or considers ridiculous. Calling the new editor-designate 'Hinton' and 'Driscoll', he mused aloud that this development was in tune with the *Eye*'s misguided new policy of seeking the custom of yobbo readers.

With the exception of Ian Hislop, everyone – including Ingrams – laughed at Waugh's attack, delivered in the kind of regretful tones that might be employed by a duke who has just been told that he has to open his home to the public and engage a business manager.

His face now white with anger, Ian Hislop rose to reply to Waugh's barbs, which had aroused great mirth among the luncheon guests. Instead of framing his remarks with a show of good humour, he made some rather obvious points about how his generation would be writing jokes long after Waugh's had gone. It was time *Private Eye* changed, he suggested – time it found new targets and sources of comedy. Hislop's angry contempt, and his impatience with the old teasing ways in which *Eye* rows are usually conducted, did not find favour. In an absurd way, some of those present felt threatened. The old jokes were going to be changed, and we reacted like pensioners in a retirement home who have suddenly been offered filthy foreign food.

The luncheon had scarcely ended before Silvester and Halloran were on the telephone, selling the story to the newspapers; later in the afternoon Ingrams composed an announcement for the Press Association news agency.

My own contribution to the debate was to question if Ingrams really meant to go. Did he really propose to leave the magazine?, I asked. Ingrams said he would be coming in for two days during the 'on' week, plus the publishing Monday. He said he was tired of the train journeys, and of Norman Balon's Coach and Horses food, and that he wanted to concentrate on writing books.

Why, in that case, did he want to come in at all? Why not leave altogether? Ingrams said he wished to continue contributing to the magazine, but that he wanted Ian to take over things like 'speaking to lawyers'. He left the luncheon table, followed by Hislop, saying there was nothing more to discuss. Next day and on Sunday the papers carried long stories about the lunch. The story was considered newsworthy enough for 'News At Ten'. *The Sunday Times* carried a report on the front page, with a picture of Hislop and a headline: 'The *Eye* fumes over its new "midget" editor'. Nigel Dempster was quoted as saying of Hislop: 'I don't think people like midgets, especially pushy midgets. I think he is a deeply unpleasant little man. He is the one and only reason that I left the *Eye* last year.'

Dempster, who was later rebuked for his 'midget' comments in a magazine for disabled people, had severed his thirteen-year association with the *Eye* in 1985, following the hullaballoo over a story about former Tory Cabinet Minister Cecil Parkinson's affairs. Parkinson had earlier resigned from the Cabinet after admitting that he was the father of a child by his former secretary, Sara Keays. In March 1985 *Private Eye* carried a 'Grovel' story suggesting he was now carrying on an affair with his new secretary. Parkinson heard that this was to appear before the magazine came out, and he applied successfully for an injunction.

Dempster was accused of writing the story in 'Grovel'. But he claimed the item had been 'shown' to him at *Private Eye*, and that he had advised against publishing it unless it could be thoroughly checked. Hislop's recollection is quite different. He says Dempster wrote the story, handed it in – and said nothing of any further checking until the row blew up. Ingrams believed Hislop.

Dempster told Ingrams he would not work for the *Eye* again unless Hislop was fired. Ingrams refused to do this, believing that Dempster would cool down and return to the fold. But this did not happen, and Ingrams concluded that Dempster had been badly frightened by the row. An emotional Dempster had called Ingrams to say: '*Private Eye* is succeeding where Goldsmith failed – it will get me sacked from the *Mail*.'

The Parkinson story had been investigated at the *Daily Mail*, where Dempster had been writing a gossip column for more than ten years. And the editor, Sir David English, knew that *Mail* reporters had been checking out a tip about a new Parkinson romance. But Sir David had also had the opportunity of talking personally to Parkinson, and he had been assured by the ex-Minister that there was no substance to the story.

Then it appeared in *Private Eye*. Parkinson was tipped off by a *Daily Mail* reporter that the story was about to appear, which is how he was able to go swiftly into action with an injunction that enabled him to force *Private Eye* to remove all references to him from all but the subscription copies. It appeared to Ingrams that *Private Eye* had been used by *Daily Mail* journalists to float a story so that Parkinson's reaction could be solicited without danger to the *Mail*. They had not anticipated that his reaction would be so dramatic. However, it made a front page story – and one without risk to the *Daily Mail*.

So Ingrams penned a special 'Gnome' leader comment in the *Eye* naming Dempster as the author of the Parkinson story. Now, a year later, Dempster had a new opportunity to vent his feelings about Hislop – who he still felt had come close to losing him his *Daily Mail* job. Dempster told *The Sunday Times*: 'He knows nothing about journalism. He is not a journalist in any shape, size or form. And *Private Eye* is essentially about journalism.' *The Sunday Times* account added: 'Dempster made other unflattering remarks about Hislop which, for legal reasons, cannot be reported.'

Another unnamed 'opponent' of Hislop told *The Sunday Times*: 'Hislop is an absolutely ludicrous figure. I can't tell you how aggressive he is. It's nonsense for him to say he represents the young. He is the personification of Middle-Aged Man. He wears baggy tweed trousers. He's balding and bespectacled. He drinks half pints at lunchtime. He's overweight. He has what he would call a steady relation-ship.'

The 'opponent' was easily identifiable as Jane Ellison, a part-time *Eye* reporter and former favourite of Ingrams. Her dislike of Hislop was well known at the *Eye*.

After the furore, Ingrams departed for Berkshire and Hislop left on a skiing holiday in Verbier. But indignation continued to mount among the staff, contributors, ex-contributors – and even shareholders. The majority share-holder, with sixty-eight per cent of the shares, is the comedian Peter Cook. He was contacted by David Cash and a meeting was fixed to discuss the Hislop news.

Peter Cook said he was not surprised that Ingrams wanted to take it easy after twenty-three years 'of non-stop litigation'. But, he added: 'I think there is no reason why staff who have also worked there for a long time should not be consulted. I am available if they want to ring me up.'

Cash told *The Sunday Times* that he personally was 'far from happy', and that the new appointment could be blocked. He said: 'I can dig my heels in if I want to. My view is that Hislop should run the funny side of the magazine, but that we need someone with more experience to run the serious side of things. That would alleviate the problem that Hislop does not have the backing of the hacks. The one thing that Hislop could not do as editor is hire and fire staff. He does not have the authority.'

My own published contribution to the initial debate was in the *Mail on Sunday*, where I offered the view that Ingrams' retirement was 'a sham'. I also drew attention to his tyrannical method of appointing a successor, which would not have seemed out of place in an *Eye* story in the 'Street of Shame' column.

Personally, I told Ingrams that I thought the Hislop criticism was misplaced, and that my own attack on him was based on the principle that there was no point in dealing with the monkey if the organ grinder was present. He seemed to take it in good enough part. We have often aimed arrows at each other in print. Then he said: 'You're fired.'

'Right,' I replied.

For reasons unconnected with the row I did not go into the *Eye* office for a couple of days. When colleagues asked if I had been fired I told them I had. Then Ingrams called: 'I hear you have been saying you're fired,' he said.

'Haven't I?' I asked with a laugh.

'Of course not – get in here,' he replied.

Nigel Dempster now arranged a special luncheon, with my help, at the Gay Hussar. The principal guest was to be Peter Cook. I put a paragraph announcing this notable event into my *Standard* column due to appear on the morning of the lunch:

> Today, *Private Eye*'s new editor-designate, Ian Hislop, takes his seat after a skiing holiday abroad, and an interesting new era begins at our most ballyhooed magazine. He faces the difficult task of supplanting a man who, for three days a week, will remain on the premises. I have suggested to the majority shareholder, Peter Cook, that he sack Ingrams – cast him off with a large pension and a gold watch into the Berkshire backwaters to which the old bibliophile says he is so devoted. This would give Wee Hislop a chance to establish himself outside the shadow of Ingrams' massive ego. Today there is to be a Soho lunch at which this suggestion will be discussed. I don't expect anything will come of it, but the occasion just might shame the old tyrant off to the Shires for good.

We assembled in the top-floor private room of the Gay Hussar – Peter Cook, Auberon Waugh, Patrick Marnham,

David Cash, Nigel Dempster, Dick West and myself. Dempster then made what was generally believed afterwards to have been a crucial mistake. He invited Waugh to choose the wine. After fastidiously studying the list, Bron opted for Gressier Grand Poujeaux Haut Médoc at twenty-five pounds a bottle. Cook's enthusiasm for the wine was no greater, but certainly no less, than everyone else's. The difficulty was that, although he was not then aware of it, he would have urgent business to attend to after lunch.

The general view was that Hislop could not fill Ingrams' shoes and that Ingrams' manner of announcing his departure – at the leaving party of a popular colleague – was insensitive. Waugh said he did not mind this in the least. But he reiterated his view that under Hislop jokes would be calculated to appeal to a yobbo audience, and that the successful *Private Eye* had no need of such people.

Dempster urged the view that Hislop was not a proper journalist, and did not understand how stories were gathered, written and used to proper advantage. He should be fired. Dick West raised the suspicion that Hislop might seek to suck up to minorities such as feminists and homosexuals, whose proselytizing activities had long provided *Private Eye* with targets for satire. David Cash confirmed that Hislop did not enjoy the confidence of any of the *Eye* staff except the editor.

Cook enjoyed the wine and occasionally lightened the atmosphere with jokes. My own expressed view was that it was undesirable for Ingrams to have been allowed to choose his successor, and certainly not without reference to his fellow directors, shareholders and senior colleagues.

By appointing his own successor and staying on in an undefined capacity, Ingrams was making life easier for himself and more difficult for his colleagues. By now several bottles of fine claret had come and gone, and there was a call for some kind of decision to be made.

Cook pronounced himself willing to confront Ingrams if we could decide on what he should say. Dick West suggested that Hislop should be put in charge of the 'funnies', and that I be appointed editor of the rest of the magazine. Cash asked if I would serve if I was called, and I said I would. There was a call for a show of hands, and I was happy to receive the unanimous blessing of my merry luncheon friends. Waugh said, feelingly: 'I'd follow him like a dog.'

It was now a simple matter of Cook returning to the *Eye* with David Cash and confronting 'Ayatollah' Ingrams. I drove home to await the call to greatness. It was a long time coming. And when it did, the news was confused.

Cook and Cash had confronted Ingrams after our lunch, but Cook could not remember what passed between them. Neither could Ingrams, who said he had had difficulty 'following' Cook. Cash did manage to represent to Ingrams the view that Hislop was unqualified and unsuitable to control the 'hack' side of the magazine. But Ingrams treated the 'Chief Box Wallah' to one of his blue, basilisk stares, and the matter was fudged. Hislop agreed to invite Paul Foot to lunch, presumably in the hope of receiving a crash course in *Eye* journalism. The Gressier Grand Poujeaux had done its work.

An account of the lunch appeared in *Eye* 634 under the heading 'Angry Scenes Outside Gnome House, By Our man in Soho Gay Hussar'. It linked our revolt with the striking printers outside Murdoch's plant in Wapping.

Hundreds of enraged ex-*Private Eye* employees (Sid and Doris Dumpster) yesterday held a mass-lunch to protest at the 'savage redundancies' recently imposed by Lord Gnome. As the massed ranks of pickets lurched out of one of Soho's leading eateries, the swanky £50 a head Chez Victor Sassie, they shouted 'Give us back our jobs, you Fascist bastard.'

THIRD WORLD WAUGH

Leading the demonstration as it swayed towards the grim walls of the so called 'Fortress Satire' were several sacked former employees including Auberon Baugh, Patrick Washedup, Peter McLie and the balding increasingly insane Dumpster himself, 55. Massed ranks of police (PC Ned Strangelove) met the protest outside Gnome House, and after a few seconds managed to turn back what a bystander later described as 'this human tide of filth'. Afterwards, police put on show a display of weapons used by the demonstrators. These included a half-empty bottle of Château Combe Florey 1947, a furled copy of the *Literary Review* (slightly stained) and the remains of an expensive Cuban cigar with the personalised monogram 'P M'.

YESTERDAY'S MEN

A sobbing Mr Baugh told me: 'We have ruthlessly resigned from our jobs and now we want them back.'

Another senior demonstrator, Mr Richard Pist, said: 'I don't know who wash paying for thish lunch, but it wash jolly good.'

Lord Rothermere is £249 worse off.

Jane Ellison was a reporter on the London *Standard* whose articles had caught Ingrams' eye in 1979. He had asked her to the *Private Eye* lunch, then invited her to contribute to the magazine. They enjoyed a warm, bantering relationship. But it was not to survive the Hislop appointment.

Jane had left the staff of the *Standard* to go freelance, with the *Eye* being her principal source of regular income while she wrote her first novel. Her relationship with Hislop prior to his elevation had been abrasive – but not, she thought, unmanageable. They traded genial insults. Even after she fell under suspicion of supplying anti-Hislop quotes to *The Sunday Times* in the wake of the l'Escargot luncheon, they continued to work together. But the atmosphere darkened. Ian Hislop felt uncomfortable about Jane's relationship with Ingrams. After one Coach and Horses lunch he exploded to the indiscreet Silvester: 'I hate the way she sucks up to him.'

Hislop was coming under disconcerting pressure from journalists eager to profile the editor-designate of *Private Eye*. Freelance writer Jessica Berens had been to see him for *The Sunday Times* magazine, and a rumour got about that she had got it into her head that he was a homosexual. Given the *Eye*'s reputation for 'hounding the pooves', it might indeed have been news if the new editor was a member of this despised minority. But it was untrue, and as embarrassing to Miss Berens as it was to Hislop.

Another lady profiler, Val Hennessy, wrote in the *Mail on Sunday*'s *You* magazine what was considered to be a demolition job on Hislop, which included asking him if he was a homosexual. He said he wasn't, but she left the question and answer in anyway.

Meanwhile, Jane Ellison had been invited by Auberon Waugh to contribute to the *Literary Review*. The mischievous Waugh thought she might start by writing an anonymous piece about the *Eye*, and in particular Waugh's new figure of fun, 'Hinton'.

Waugh then leaked the gist of this piece to his friend Geoffrey Wheatcroft – himself an *Eye* figure of fun – the editor of the *Standard*'s 'Londoner's Diary' column. The story appeared the day before one of the fortnightly *Eye* luncheons at the Coach and Horses.

For years Jane had been a regular at these affairs – and when Ingrams began to think they should be more formal it was Jane who typed up and put down the placement cards. As a regular *Eye* contributor she could put herself down for the lunch by writing her name in the book kept by Maggie in which the coming week's guests were recorded. She put herself down, expecting the lunch to include some questioning about the contents of her *Literary Review* piece.

On the day before the lunch she was telephoned at home by Ingrams, who began by saying: 'I see you have put yourself down for the lunch.' Anticipating a teasing about the *Literary Review* piece, she breezily replied to the effect that she could face the music. But Ingrams was not in a joking mood. He told her that it was up to him who came to the *Private Eye* lunches. 'Do you think you ought to come?' Jane thought he was joking: of course she would come.

Ingrams then got to the point. Jane recalls that he said bluntly: 'I don't think you should come. This piece of yours is going to upset a lot of people.' Jane remembers protesting: 'But I thought you'd find it funny,' to which Ingrams replied: '*Private Eye*'s a team.'

She was then told that she should not come into the

office, far less the lunch. She could not expect Ian Hislop to put up with her attacks, even if they were couched in humorous terms, 'because he's not like us'. She remembers the conversation ending with Ingrams saying: 'You have written yourself out of the script. So farewell, Jane Ellison.'

Jane Ellison said the following day: 'I could not believe he was speaking to me like this. After all these years. He knew I used to attack Ian. He even encouraged it in the past.'

In conversation with me, Ingrams denied that Jane had been sacked. But he said: 'I don't see how she can go on because she can't get on with Ian.' He then went on to say he was 'worried about Bron': 'I think he might easily turn against the *Eye*. He's in a strange mood, and I can see him making the *Eye* a target.' Sacked or not, Jane Ellison drifted back to the *Eye* after a few weeks.

Halloran's view of the Hislop succession drama was typically equivocal. The New Zealander keeps a distance between himself and Ingrams, and was amused by the atmosphere of outrage following the Hislop-to-be-editor announcement. Not that he supported Hislop's claim to the throne, either. Halloran makes a point of going his own way, choosing the stories he wants to do and fighting anyone who gets in his way. He revelled in the reaction of both Silvester and Jane Ellison, and for weeks burned up the telephones to Fleet Street with fresh gossip – and in some cases outright fabrications – about the row.

Jane Ellison, often reduced almost to tears in the past by Halloran's bullying – to which her husband, *Guardian* deputy editor Peter Cole, took particular exception – looked on the burly Antipodean as an ally in her squabble with Hislop. In her *Literary Review* article she sounded almost affectionate:

> Halloran is a robust commentator on office politics, and has ruined many of Silvester's sycophantic exchanges with the editor by shouting: 'Bend over, Richard, Christopher wants to kiss your arse!' at the critical moment.

A specialist in homosexuals, whom he refers to as 'arse bandits', and gay vicars, Halloran's primitive and earthy nature has endeared him to a stream of sultry and languid women, who pour into Carlisle Street for intimate afternoon confessions – to the envy of his colleagues. Speculation about Halloran's ability to charm beautiful women is a source of constant *Eye* gossip; the conclusion is that his particular form of rough simplicity, 'Come here, darling, would you like to sit on my dick!' proves irresistible.

Possibly thinking that it might divert suspicion elsewhere, Miss Ellison attacked herself in the *Literary Review* piece, but chose to attribute the criticism to Halloran:

If allowed to sack anyone, however, there is no doubt that Hislop would immediately rid himself of Jane Ellison, the *Eye*'s resident harpy, an unpleasant and disagreeable failed hackette, who – according to Halloran – has 'venom running through her veins'.

Ingrams said of Hislop: 'He's the only one I have ever been able to trust running the magazine. He ran it when I went on a trip to Venice with A. J. P. Taylor, and again when I went on holiday to Malta.'

Others have filled in for Ingrams when he has taken an 'on week' off over the years. Booker was 'disastrous' because he filled the magazine with his pet obsessions of the time – environment and architecture. Marnham 'could not be trusted on his own'. Dick West, although an accomplished journalist and a fine writer, was unsatisfactory, according to Ingrams. 'He's a bit like Claud Cockburn – the facts are not the most important thing.'

What Ingrams seems to mean is that those who have stood in for him over the years – a legion of failures which has also included Malcolm Muggeridge and Alan Brien – were unsatisfactory because they could not be trusted not to deviate from the very successful formula he has laid down.

Ian Hislop is entirely trustworthy in this respect. Ingrams

also thinks Hislop will be able to cope well with the inevitable meetings with lawyers. 'He handled the Spanker case well. [BBC Head of Music Richard Somerset Ward threatened *Private Eye* with a libel action when they accused him of offending women employees by discussing how they might be spanked for disobedience. He dropped the case before it came to court.] He dealt with that from start to finish. So it's no good people saying he can't cope with hack's stuff.'

There are other respects in which Ian Hislop is an ideal candidate for the position of editor: he can live in Ingrams' shadow; he has a career outside *Private Eye* composing satirical programmes for radio and television; even the all-important prerequisite of an editor, a desk, would not present a problem – the matter was discussed and David Cash said: 'Ian will sit at Richard's desk on the days Richard is not there.'

David Cash's principal objection to Hislop was that he was a threat to stability. With the magazine levelling off at a sales figure of around 250,000, Cash was concerned that nothing should disturb the surface of the editorial pond.

There is always a delicate relationship between a magazine and its readers, even an extraordinary organ like *Private Eye*. Readers might sense a falling off in the jokes or the stories, but they won't know for sure (and, more importantly, won't act on their suspicions) until they see or hear a piece of news about the magazine that could explain the drop in quality – such as that it was now under the control of a new man.

Hislop was appointed editor and assumed editorial responsibilities. But he is perhaps unique among editors of major publications in his lack of perks and dignities. His insurance stamps are not paid and his earnings are not subject to PAYE. He is not a member of the *Private Eye* pension scheme, nor does he enjoy the benefits of a company car (Ingrams had a company Metro). He is not a director, neither does he have any shares.

It is possible to view the appointment of Hislop as a mere

ruse to take the pressure off Ingrams while allowing him to continue to be in control.

Nigel Dempster sniped at Ingrams several times over the Hislop appointment, pointing out that the 'pustulous' re-tiring editor would be taking home the handsome sum of £40,000 a year for working three days a fortnight.

After my *Mail on Sunday* story saying that the Ingrams retirement was 'a sham', David Cash admitted to me that he thought this was correct. Ingrams would remain in overall control, and Ian Hislop had in reality been appointed as an assistant editor.

Ingrams told me his tiredness was genuine, and that he believed he would make a much better contribution to the jokes department if he was under less pressure to take decisions over stories and libel cases.

'You can't really make jokes if you are tired.'

Jokes have always been the cement that holds *Private Eye* together. Few of its major attacks on public figures would ever have been supported, or succeeded, if they had not been accompanied by a barrage of witticisms, irony and farce.

But *Private Eye* is also a serious business enterprise. In late 1986 the magazine, with its associated publishing and dis-tribution enterprises, is grossing a turnover of over £3 million a year, and its hold on an audience of more than one million readers is considered secure.

Early pitfalls have turned into strengths. Because of its 'scurrilous' character, it was assumed that no conventional advertisers would wish to use it. So, unlike the con-ventional press, it has never relied on income from ad-vertising – only some ten per cent of its revenue initially came from that source. Then *Private Eye* became massively popular – especially with the high-income A and B groups beloved of advertisers – and a lively demand for advertising space grew up. But the early Ingrams rules prevailed: ad-vertising would be totally separate from editorial, and it would always take up less than fifteen per cent of the space.

Private Eye's early problems with distribution were also ultimately to strengthen the magazine. W. H. Smith and John Menzies refused to accept it, and Sir James Goldsmith, in the course of his litigation in the 1970s, issued writs against many small local distributors, designed to discourage them from stocking the *Eye*.

For this reason great efforts were made by Cash to create a new, alternative network of distributors and newsagents. This has succeeded. So when W. H. Smith and John Menzies finally relented, the *Eye* was already a thriving enterprise. Nevertheless, their decision finally to stock it boosted sales by nearly 50,000 copies a fortnight.

Under Ingrams, every problem facing the *Eye* has been resolved by a combination of bold defiance and humour. Ever since its earliest defeat in the libel courts against Lord Russell of Liverpool – whom they called 'Lord Liver of Cesspool' – the *Eye* has bombarded its opponents with crude jokes, nicknames and satire. Jokes are the quills on the back of Ingrams the porcupine. He uses them to infuriate enemies and to disarm indignant friends. They are his favoured means of protection against 'bores', a vast multitude of people ranging from genuine eye-glazers to anyone saying things he does not wish to hear.

He has used a combination of shrewd, swift, private decision-making and outrageous public humour to outflank all would-be usurpers of his authority since 1963, the year he abruptly replaced Christopher Booker as editor of *Private Eye* when the latter took a long holiday.

The departure of Waugh had been handled with jokes: first, the one about Waugh being sacked; then the printing of anti-Waugh readers' letters with such headings as 'Waugh's a baugh' and 'The end of the Waugh'.

Ingrams' own retirement was portrayed as a joke, too. Tired of trains, lawyers and Norman's food, he deserved a rest from them after twenty-three years at the helm. There had been crises, but these were often dramatised for the press's benefit because the resultant publicity would swell circulation figures, not to mention profits.

Ingrams had also perfected a ploy which no conventional newspaper or magazine would have dared try on its readers. This was to set up emergency funds to pay *Private Eye*'s libel costs. In effect, this was asking readers to pay for *Private Eye*'s mistakes. But the campaigns had the further effect of enlisting moral as well as financial support, since contributors had their names printed in *Private Eye*

The one started to pay for two legal actions brought by *Observer* journalist Nora Beloff was called the Ballsoff Fund. It raised £1,282.75, modest in comparison with the Goldenballs Fund, which raised £40,000 to help with the loss of more than £1,000,000 in costs and damages incurred during the fight with financier Sir James Goldsmith – £5,000 of it contributed by the tycoon Rowland 'Tiny' Rowland of Lonrho.

Ingrams wrote in *Goldenballs* his account of the Goldsmith litigation: '. . . the *Eye* emerged as a much stronger force, aware that in an emergency it could rely on support from all sorts of unexpected quarters'.

From the earliest days Ingrams has received the encouragement and support of many influential Fleet Street journalists – although the 'Street of Shame' has also provided a fair proportion of litigants against the *Eye*. The ridicule Ingrams directed against the *Eye*'s first big legal enemy, Lord Russell of Liverpool, was taken up in Fleet Street. *Private Eye* had drawn attention to the fact that Russell's famous book, *The Scourge of the Swastika*, was offered for sale in seedy shops which dealt in pornography. They went on to suggest that its lurid detail of Nazi atrocities was designed to appeal to perverts.

In 1966, Russell won his case. Quentin Crewe, then a columnist on the *Sunday Mirror*, wrote:

The gaiety of nations took a sorry swipe when Lord Russell of Liverpool was awarded five thousand pounds libel damages against *Private Eye* . . . *Private Eye* is a scurrilous rag in the best tradition of British lampooning. It lays about authority and pomp with the vigour of the eighteenth-century pamphleteers and the Victorian cartoonists. It is a healthy pimple on the skin of an exuberant nation.

Crewe was one of the first observers to notice a unique and important attribute of *Private Eye*. He wrote:

> Many regular readers think something said in *Private Eye* quite different from something said in a serious national newspaper. The sad thing to my mind is that Lord Russell did not do so.

In 1972 *Observer* political journalist Nora Beloff brought two cases against *Private Eye*. She won one and lost one – and as a result she ended a reasonably distinguished career as a pathetic figure of fun.

Private Eye had printed a private memorandum she sent to her editor suggesting that she write a favourable article about Tory politician Reginald Maudling, then in the process of being harried by the *Eye* over questionable business dealings and associates. Auberon Waugh had made joking references to Miss Beloff – a lady of mature years, plain appearance and decidedly unflirtatious manner – suggesting she made a habit of sleeping around with senior politicians in order to get information.

Miss Beloff sued for breach of copyright in the matter of the memo, and lost. But she was successful in the matter of the Waugh libel, and won £3,000 in damages. The *Eye* and its friends were able to suggest that she was a ridiculous old woman.

Bernard Levin wrote in *The Times* that Miss Beloff's legal counsel, by keeping a straight face while outlining her case, demonstrated 'a degree of muscular control so powerful that if he should ever tire of exercising his jaw at the Bar he could successfully set up in business with it as a jobbing nutcracker'. He likened Miss Beloff's case to that of a certain Mr William Lewis Rowland Paul Sebastion Blennerhassett, 'who sued a firm of yo-yo manufacturers because in an advertisement they had invented a character Blennerhassett who became so devoted to the practice of yo-yo that he eventually had to be removed to the funny farm by the men in white coats'.

Private Eye's greatest enemy, Sir James Goldsmith, won a legal battle but lost the war. In 1979 he started a news magazine, *Now!*, which became a fortnightly target for *Eye* stories and jokes.

The stories were always to the effect that *Now!*'s sales figures were being exaggerated to attract advertising, and the running joke was that extravagant efforts were being made by Goldsmith to hide the unsold copies.

At that time, Chrysler had changed its name to Talbot, thinking this more traditional British marque might improve sales figures. *Private Eye* announced that *Now!* was to be called *Talbot* for the same reason. Every issue there would be a new *Talbot* lampoon. Following press reports about the Bermuda Triangle, the *Eye* announced that there was a 'Talbot Triangle'. Scientists had discovered the existence of a 'vast undersea mountain of unsold *Talbot* magazines' on which shipping had foundered. The *Eye*'s 'Focus on Fact' cartoon strip – a device in which defamatory biographies were produced of *Eye* enemies – was devoted for months to an exploration of every single manifestation of the name *Talbot*.

Readers and contributors complained that the joke was no longer funny. Ingrams said such complaints made the joke even more risible. 'I think the *Talbot* days were among the *Eye*'s funniest,' he said in 1986.

The effect of the joke was devastating among the advertising and media people who had to deal with *Now!*. There were stories of how meetings held to discuss *Now!* disintegrated into hilarity when *Talbot* was mentioned. The eventual outcome of *Private Eye*'s gleeful campaign was that *Now!* went down with all hands, losing more than £20 million, with the jeers of its Greek Street tormentors ringing in the ears of its captain, Sir James Goldsmith. As a viable publishing property the magazine was never considered to have hit its stride. But it had also been laughed to death.

Private Eye's unique formula calls for a double-barrelled

attack on those targeted as enemies. They are clobbered with unhelpful disclosures in the news section, then speared in the 'funnies'. The jokes have the effect of both legitimising the attack and disarming the victims. This is an Ingrams recipe, and rightly or wrongly the majority of those who contribute to *Private Eye* believe that only Ingrams understands the combustible formula, and in other less experienced hands it would be dangerous. Ingrams has been through long legal wars, and is seen to have suffered. In one Goldsmith case – an attempt to deploy old criminal libel laws – he was faced with the prospect of going to prison. He is credited with having shown courage in the face of wealthy and powerful enemies.

He is a respectable public figure, a sought-after radio and TV broadcaster, the guru of generations of young journalists, and a man whose friendship has been sought by eminent people, such as former Master of the Rolls Lord Denning and Graham Greene.

Yet for the first time since Ingrams took control of the magazine in 1963, fundamental questions were being raised about how the magazine was run at the time of his retirement. *Private Eye* has never paid a dividend to shareholders. If there is any profit after the bills have been paid it is shared among the staff and regular contributors in the form of bonus payments. If *Private Eye* were to succeed in reducing its libel bill, which became a serious objective in 1986, the magazine could easily make profits of around £250,000 a year. Would profits continue to be distributed among the staff and contributors?

Private Eye does not have a board and directors, and there are no conventional board meetings as such. Decisions have always been taken by Ingrams in consultation with Cash. In 1986 it was agreed that paging should be increased to thirty-two with nine of them set aside for advertising. Earlier configurations had been twenty-four/six and twenty-eight/seven. The price also rose from forty to forty-five pence.

Cecilia Boggis, who had been engaged to operate the IBM

typesetting machines, was put in charge of the small ads. *Private Eye* has always favoured small ads over display advertising because the former, which include personal and lonely hearts messages, have more editorial appeal, and are more in keeping with the collegiate tone of the magazine than display ads for Macallan Scotch and Jack Daniels Tennessee Whisky.

One regular display ad did have the ideal resonance – the one for 'the dazzling new 1986 citroen 2CV Dolly. £3,149'. This car is much favoured among people on low incomes, and the *Eye* advertising was appropriately unpretentious.

> After considerable restraint, we've finally splashed out on our endearing little runabout. Not on its advertising, mind. Only on its wings. Bright green wings for the 2CV Dolly on top. (Very fetching with the white, don't you think?) And bright red wings for the Dolly below. In other ways, of course, it's the same old story. Interiors that remain reassuringly sparse. Petrol consumption that remains reassuringly miserly. And an engine compartment that remains reassuringly empty. (There's still more space than engine, so there's still less to service or repair.) At Citroen, you see, we've always relied on our car to sell our car. Never on glossy advertising.

The ad, with small changes, might well have been written for *Private Eye* itself. There have been twenty-five years of considerable restraint on the marketing (if not the editorial) side; the interior remains reassuringly sparse; and no reliance whatsoever is made on glossy advertising.

By contrast, *Punch* appears to rely wholly on selling itself with expensive television and newspaper advertising campaigns. Even the staid old *Spectator* magazine is now printed on glossy paper and carries colour illustrations; it too is advertised on television.

Yet despite their dazzlingly colourful looks – or perhaps because of them – there is no appreciable market for back copies of either *Punch* or the *Spectator*. A full set of *Eyes*, in mint condition, might fetch anything from £5,000 to £10,000 in 1986.

But the modest price, and appearance, of the magazine has not been dictated entirely by Ingrams' unpretentious nature, nor by his horror of modern contrivances and marketing theories.

'We have left *Punch* standing,' says Ingrams. 'In the old days *Punch* had a circulation of 124,000. Now it is 65,000 and it has gone over to the glossy advertising game. We no longer regard *Punch* as a rival.'

Private Eye has to look amateur, especially now that its sales and profits have risen so dramatically. Although it has never been acknowledged, it might even have been necessary from time to time to lose money in legal damages and costs. The reason for this lies in *Private Eye*'s position close to the frontiers of acceptability. In its savage pursuit of those Ingrams sees as liars and humbugs, it has littered the streets with bleeding casualties – sometimes innocent bystanders. Even its most self-righteous readers must have had occasional qualms about this carnage. So *Private Eye*'s periodical thrashings in the courts – themselves valuable in terms of publicity – have the paradoxical effect of encouraging wider acceptance. Like a watchdog which has erred and been thoroughly beaten for it, *Private Eye*'s relationship with its readers grows stronger when there is seen to be a legal check on its excesses.

Does Ian Hislop understand *Private Eye*? He told Val Hennessy in their interview about the l'Escargot lunch: 'I remained calm and told them of my intentions to find satirical targets to appeal to younger readers. I also pointed out that if the old guard don't like me as editor, that's their funeral. I revealed my plan to cut the spiralling costs of libel actions and I hinted at certain exciting future plans for the *Eye*.'

His future 'hit list' would include Jonathan King, Roger Daltrey, Terry Wogan and Peter York. He also has what Miss Hennessy called 'violent satirical plans for Samantha Fox'. Hislop has said of Miss Fox, who became famous by displaying her large breasts in the *Sun*:

She's certainly worth a turnover. My antagonism dates from when I was on a Radio 4 programme with her and she was given five minutes to air her views on charity. The fact is, Samantha Fox has big tits and that's all. Why people should be interested in her views on charity I don't know . . . Oh God, she was so awful, a dithering, coquettish parody of sexuality. Please note that this is not a prudish objection. I like sexy women as much as the next man, but she, like Mrs Thatcher, is quite ludicrous.

Hennessy was brutal:

If the glory of youth glows in Hislop's soul then there isn't much sign of it as he witters on about his mortgage, his bachelor flat in Clapham, and his Dire Straits albums.

Hislop told *City Limits* magazine that he intends to broaden *Private Eye*'s appeal. 'Spitting Image' had taught him that satire is capable of reaching a large audience. With his cartoonist friend Nick Newman, Hislop writes up-to-the-minute sketches which are recorded on the day the show goes out. Puppet maker Roger Law acknowledges the influence of *Private Eye* on the show. He said in an interview with *Sounds* in April:

There is a much firmer tradition of taking the piss out of people in power in this country compared to others . . . *Private Eye* you couldn't say is a left-wing magazine, it's some sort of weird Tory anarchist thing, yet the people who buy it come from all walks of life, from unemployed people through to Cabinet Ministers. Having that tradition of satire obviously helps you.

'Spitting Image' is a milder commercial production than *Private Eye*. There is no serious intention behind its jokes – other than to ridicule people who appear regularly on TV and in the papers. Indeed, what it tends to ridicule is the newspaper image of the personality involved. Hence the unsupported view of the tabloid newspapers that the Princess of Wales bullies Prince Charles, and that the

Queen feuds with Princess Michael of Kent, is grist to their mill. Producer John Lloyd goes out of his way to explain that he likes and admires the Queen, and that it is all done in the most affectionate possible spirit. Of course it is.

Ian Hislop's view of satire is similarly lightweight. He is not a hater like Ingrams, or if he is he reserves his animosity for insubstantial figures such as Samantha Fox and Jonathan King. While Ingrams broods about politicians, church leaders, business tycoons and media barons, looking for clues that they have betrayed the principles by which they secured their eminence, Ian Hislop's deeper concerns have not made themselves apparent.

But Ingrams now gives the appearance of a man who has fought his major battles, and now wants to retire to the less fraught pages of the funnies. Yet the success of the non-satirical sections of *Private Eye* depends largely on the anger and desire of the editor in charge to expose wickedness, and to communicate his rage to contributors. The temptation facing Ian Hislop will be to tone down the front and back sections of the magazine as a way of trimming 'the spiralling costs of libel actions'.

'It is a no-alternative choice,' says Ingrams. 'There is no one else. Hislop has been groomed for the job. We have to make changes. I shall keep a big foot in the door. The *Eye* is a terrific business success. I am not a good businessman in the conventional sense. But I have helped to create a profitable business. It is still unexploited in its potential.'

Auberon Waugh wrote in the *Spectator* after Ingrams' announcement:

The great point about Richard Ingrams is that he is extremely funny and has used his sense of the ridiculous as well as his powers of parody to create an alternative perception of life in Britain which has had a profound effect on the nation's awareness of itself throughout the last quarter of a century . . . It may just be a healthy middle-aged man's hatred of the young which makes me suppose that *Private Eye* will now degenerate into a teenage comic or disintegrate under the pressure of innumerable libel suits . . . my generation must feel sad that Ingrams has decided to throw in the sponge after so many years, even as we marvel that he held it so long. Of all my contemporaries, he is undoubtedly the one who has made the greatest mark on his times.

For good measure, Auberon Waugh informed his local paper, the *Western Daily Press*: 'I don't think he [Hislop] has the strength of character for the job.'

It was perhaps strange that Hislop played no part in the power struggle that followed Ingrams' announcement. Dave Cash was one of those who moved quickly to strengthen their own positions. Ingrams' decision to stay on as chairman and three-day-a-fortnight joke contributor might have meant that was less for Cash to do. Ingrams has always felt that *Eye* staff should be part-time, but this was in part self-serving. Ingrams, because he was known as editor of the *Eye*, found it quite easy to pick up other work – writing books, contributing articles, and broadcasting on radio and television. That course was not open to the little-known Cash, nor for that matter to Tony Rushton. But Ingrams was able privately to assure Cash that nothing much would change.

There were no other contenders for the Hislop job, whatever it was to be. From the earliest days, Ingrams has always been quite ruthless about his control of the magazine, and since he will remain chairman he is unlikely to let that control go now. Some old *Eye* hands still remember with resentment his coup in 1962, when he literally locked editor Christopher Booker out of the office. Elizabeth Luard, wife of the *Eye*'s business wizard Nicholas Luard, told me in 1986 that she thought Ingrams 'an extraordinarily ruthless man'.

Mrs Luard is of the view that Ingrams is to a great extent influenced by his wife, Mary. She remembers an incident in the 1960s involving the old *Eye* office in Neal Street, Covent Garden:

We had this office on sufferance from a businessman who was not particularly nice. But he put up with us on condition that we locked the premises when we left each night because his warehouse was at the back. One night Richard and Mary, who was then the secretary, stayed late in the office, and forgot to lock it. Next day the man who owned it was absolutely furious, demanding an explanation as to why we had failed to do the one thing he had insisted should be done. Richard and Mary absolutely refused to do anything about it. They wouldn't even see him, far less apologise. It was left to me, the silly deb, to go cringing to the man and take the blame. He shouted and ranted at me, almost reducing me to tears. I just hung my head and took it.

Mrs Luard worked closely with Mary at the *Eye* offices, and remembers that the Irish girl was mad about Ingrams:

He wasn't interested in women at all. Lots of very attractive women loved him, but he just wasn't interested. Mary stuck to him like glue. She was quite rich, and rather obsessed by money. She said to me once: 'How much are you worth?' I had no idea. She said she was worth £100,000, which was then a lot of money – probably the equivalent of a million now.

But it never occurred to Mary to give any money to *Private Eye*, and that was true of Richard, too. They thought other people should put the money up. I was always a greater fan of Booker than I was of Richard. Booker really is a good man, but I am afraid I have always thought Richard devious.

Chapter Three

Happy Ship

Who's Who modestly describes itself as 'the recognised source book of information on people of influence and interest in all fields'; the 1986 edition, and in particular Nigel Dempster's entry, also turned out to be the source of one of the most absurd rows in *Private Eye*'s history.

Nigel Richard Patton Dempster's career provides him with a most dazzling entry. It tells of his two marriages, and of his early career as an insurance broker with Lloyds of London and on the Stock Exchange. It mentions his three years as a PR account executive with the Earl of Kimberley Associates, then goes on to recount his long career in journalism, with the *Daily Express*, the *Daily Mail*, *Status* magazine (USA), *Queen* and *Private Eye*. For good measure Dempster also describes himself as a broadcaster with the ABC network in the USA and with CBC in Canada, and records that he is the author of a biography of Princess Margaret – *HRH The Princess Margaret – A Life Unfulfilled*. He lists his recreations as photography, squash and running marathons, and his clubs as the Automobile and the Chappaquiddick Beach in Massachusetts.

It is a long and impressive entry. But there are curious elements in it, and these would earn the close scrutiny of Fleet Street colleagues, newspaper diarists and magazine editors across London. As a diarist on the *Express*, the *Mail* and *Private Eye*, Nigel Dempster had, after all, become the arch-scrutineer of English society, the King of Gossip Columnists. Now that he was a man of 'influence' or 'interest', how would he present himself among the ranks of those he had been writing about for more than two decades?

To the millions who have seen him on television, or have read his column in the *Daily Mail*, Nigel Dempster is a sleek, dark-haired man in middle age, well-spoken and amusingly bitchy. He is seemingly omnipresent on all occasions that involve the Royal Family, the aristocracy, and that lesser but by no means less interesting raft of public names that swim before us daily in newspapers, television, radio and films.

The entry he composed for *Who's Who* – those considered worthy of inclusion are sent forms to fill in – caused amusement partly because – like many other entries – it was as interesting for what was left out as for what was put in.

It fails to mention, for instance, that his journalistic career began not just on the *Daily Express* but on that paper's famous William Hickey column. It might have been interesting for *Who's Who* readers (particularly those who read the *Daily Mail*) to know this, since a major feature of his later *Daily Mail* diary was his derogatory references to the William Hickey column.

He had worked as number four in seniority under Richard Berens, the Old Etonian former Hussars officer who edited the Hickey column. Dempster was regarded, however, as one of the column's star reporters, known to colleagues as 'the lead machine' because of his skill in picking up gossip exciting enough to be the column's main story on the night. However, he was not universally popular in the higher echelons of the paper. Berens later recalled that he had asked Dempster if he could make his daily entrance to the office by the back stairs rather than the front because a chance meeting with the editor in the front hall would be a provocative reminder of his presence on the paper.

There was another little omission in the *Who's Who* entry which amused Dempster's friends in Fleet Street. He gave the impression that his career at the *Daily Mail* had begun as 'Editor, Mail Diary'. In fact, he had been engaged by Paul Callan, who inaugurated the *Daily Mail* diary when the paper became a tabloid in 1972. Dempster proved to be a highly energetic and ambitious number two, and within a year he had replaced Callan as diary editor.

But the most amusing feature of Dempster's *Who's Who* entry was his inclusion of a host of glittering names. It is rare for those asked to supply personal details to include the name of their ex-mother-in-law, let alone the lady's father. But Lady Patricia Douglas, daughter of the Marquess of Queensbury, is there; so too is his second mother-in-law and her second husband, Sir David Lawrence. He even found space for the name of the PR firm in which he had worked twenty-six years before – Earl of Kimberley Associates, and for mentioning his contributions to *Status* magazine.

All of this caused merriment at *Private Eye*, where Dempster's social climbing and his encyclopaedic memory for aristocratic names and details had been something of a joke for years. It seemed delightfully appropriate that the man who had spent twenty-three years poring over *Who's Who* to verify details of those he wrote about should, when asked to compose his own entry, jam it with as many names from that world as was permissible.

But the revelation most appreciated at Gnome House was that one of Dempster's family names is Pratt. Just after the 1986 *Who's Who* was published, Silvester hurried into Ingrams' office and announced that he had an excellent item for 'Grovel': 'Dempster's real name is Pratt.' By this time Dempster had been on bad terms with *Private Eye* for a year, following the Parkinson affair. Some of his friends believed he was acting like a prat, which, in modern terms of abuse, is someone with the dual characteristics of a shit and a wally.

Private Eye had been sniping gently at Dempster since his departure, saying that by his behaviour he had forfeited the former appellation accorded to him by Auberon Waugh and Ingrams – the 'Greatest Living Englishman'. There had also been teasing to the effect that the former scourge of high society was now filling his columns with favourable references to Princess Michael of Kent, whom he had recently met.

Now if Silvester was right, there was a marvellous new joke. Dempster really was a Pratt. Ingrams reacted with enthusiasm. Silvester also said he had been told by an associate of Dempster's that Pratt was not merely a middle name, but the former Greatest Living Englishman's surname. *Who's Who* was produced, and the entry was scrutinised. It said Dempster was the son of Eric Richard Pratt and Angela Grace Dempster. I pointed out that Dempster might simply have wanted to shorten the passage by not using 'Dempster' twice and that this might have to do with the house style of *Who's Who*. A study of other entries was not conclusive; but it seemed that many who had taken the course of omitting their mother's married name had placed her maiden name in brackets after her Christian names. So if Dempster's mother's maiden name had, say, been Smith, the entry would have read: 's. of Eric Richard Pratt Dempster and Angela Grace Dempster (nee Smith)'.

Silvester was not convinced but Ingrams nevertheless refused to allow the proposed 'Grovel' item to appear.

A week later the story made it to the gossip column of the *Sunday Mirror*, where, apparently, it had been accepted that Dempster's father's name really was Pratt. Dempster's lawyers contacted the *Sunday Mirror*, and a swift correction soon appeared:

MR NIGEL DEMPSTER

We suggested last week that Mr Nigel Dempster's father was someone other than Mr Eric R. P. Dempster. We now know this to be untrue. Mr and Mrs E. R. P. Dempster were happily married for 56 years until Mr Dempster's death at the age of 90 in December, 1983. We were wrong to imply that Mr Nigel Dempster, *Daily Mail* diarist, broadcaster and Royal biographer, had taken his mother's name. Our apologies to Mrs A. G. Dempster and Nigel Dempster for the distress this has caused.

This generous apology had no sooner appeared than the

story popped up again, this time in the social magazine *Ritz*. On the front cover was a teasing headline 'Is Dempster a Pratt?', and inside was an item about the confusing *Who's Who* entry. This time Dempster took more direct action. He called up *Ritz*'s editor, David Litchfield, and berated him over the telephone. Perhaps if he had known that Litchfield was tape-recording the conversation he would have left the matter to his lawyers.

In the following issue of *Ritz* a two-page 'Interview' appeared, based on the conversation and introduced: 'Nigel Dempster, by David Litchfield'.

'The following is a two act play based on our telephone conversations and entitled Pratt's Last Fall or The Ramblings Of A Man Who Doesn't Like Having Done To Him As He Does To Others . . .' Dempster began by pointing out that there were various ways of listing one's parents in *Who's Who*. 'I put my father's initials and my mother's initials and our surname . . . Therefore my father's names are Eric Richard Pratt Dempster and my mother's names are Angela Grace Dempster.' It cannot be described as a cheerful exchange. Dempster tells Litchfield at one point:

> Okay. So how are you going to pay for it? You're going to have to do something, buddy, because I'm going to take you to the f . . . . . g cleaners! This has gone on long enough. This is one of twenty incidents when you've written about me and been totally inaccurate. I've got them all on file, every single one of them, so obviously this is a malicious campaign. So I hope you realise what I'm saying to you, that every single one of them is tabulated and you are going to have to do something that satisfies me and my solicitors, and I'm ringing you up to tell you that you've made a c . . t of yourself . . . because you are a c . . t and you know you are, so I'm warning you that I want some form of recognition . . .

Ingrams greeted the *Ritz* piece jubilantly – 'Prattie's cracking up!' – and it was filed in his voluminous collection of clippings. Meanwhile, Dempster set about the task of discovering who had arranged his 'Prattfall'. Here, I must involve myself in the narrative.

Dempster and I had been friends for nearly twenty years. We lunched, dined and went to parties together. We played golf at the RAC country club at Epsom, of which Dempster is a member, and enjoyed friendly rivalry.

When I had edited the William Hickey column in the 1970s, Dempster used to snipe at our stories. He once printed an inaccurate story about my then girlfriend (now my wife) for which he had to write a letter of apology on *Daily Mail* headed paper and pay her £500 in damages. We have had several spats, but have always managed to patch them up.

When I returned from the United States at the end of 1985 we resumed our friendship; but there was a problem. I was still on friendly terms with Ingrams and I resumed my contributions to *Private Eye*. When the Pratt row broke Dempster wrote to me saying he was 'stunned to learn' that I had brought a photostat copy of his *Who's Who* entry into *Private Eye*. Because of this 'treacherous action' he could not believe me to be a friend any more.

I wrote back saying I regretted that our friendship had become a casualty of the struggles of *Private Eye*, which was true. Three days later Dempster wrote back saying it was 'beyond dispute' that I had been involved in what he called an investigation of his genealogy, adding that our friendship would not have been jeopardized if I had had the sense to recognise that the *Eye* was 'a busted flush'.

I wrote back again, suggesting among other things that he lacked a sense of proportion about the matter. Dempster's final letter spoke of my 'constant duplicity and treachery', and 'as you seem to wish to continue as Ingrams' lickspittle, you will have to be treated accordingly'.

At that time I was writing a column for the *Daily Mail's* sister paper, the *Mail on Sunday*, and I was called in by the editor, Mr Stewart Steven. In high good humour, he told me he had just received a visit from Dempster, who had suggested that I be fired. Dempster, according to Steven, had said that I wrote the *Eye*'s satirical 'Sir Jonah Junor' column which, in the spirit of the columnist it was intended to lampoon, had the week before carried an item about Steven. It was derived from a *Mail on Sunday* story suggesting that Margaret Thatcher had been dealing in shares while Prime Minister. While not actually illegal, this goes against the spirit of the rules governing the private financial dealings of Prime Ministers. 'Sir Jonah', a fervent Thatcher supporter in lampoon and reality, indignantly dismissed the *Mail on Sunday* allegations and waspishly raised the question of their provenance. Steven, he claimed, was the man responsible for 'discovering' Martin Bormann, and had also personally faked the notorious letter in the *Daily Mail*-British Leyland affair. He ended by suggesting, in characteristic Junor style, a new job for Steven – 'chief rodent operative in the sewers of Tel Aviv'.

Dempster, said Steven, had been particularly incensed by this latter insult because of its blatantly anti-Semitic character. However, Steven wished that this had been brought to his attention by someone other than Dempster. Why, I wondered?

Steven explained that while he had been an executive of the *Daily Mail* he once had subbed a Dempster story, removing what he thought might be a legally dangerous element. Dempster had responded in what Steven took to be anti-Semitic terms – so much so that the mild-mannered Steven had brought the matter to the attention of the *Daily Mail* editor, Sir David English. English, too, had been indignant, said Steven, and had called Dempster into his office.

Dempster denied that he had made anti-Semitic remarks to Steven, adding: 'I didn't even know he was a Jew – I thought he was a Turk!'

The whole ridiculous affair, it seemed to me, only served to illustrate the truth of a remark of Dr Johnson's which Ingrams much admired, and which he used as the text for the book he wrote on the Goldsmith affair, *Goldenballs*:

Few attacks either of ridicule or invective make much noise, but for the help of those that they provoke.

Dempster now became a chief figure of fun on the *Eye*'s satire pages. He figured in the list of names in the *Eye*'s 'Court circular' – 'fourth carriage, Mr Nigel Pratt-Dumpster' – and this nickname replaced his previous appelation, 'Mr Humpty Dumpster'. Ingrams delighted in the joke, even when Dempster retaliated in his *Daily Mail* column by referring to the *Eye* editor as a 'pustulous reformed alcoholic' with a 'Bohemian home life' and a wife who was 'frumpy'. Dempster also telephoned Mary at her Wallingford bookshop to tell her that the ridicule he was suffering in the *Eye* would be repaid with interest in the *Daily Mail*.

Ingrams said it was sad that the *Eye* had lost Dempster, and feared that the wounds inflicted on 'the Humpty Dumpty Man' would not soon heal. The Pratt affair enraged Dempster, overshadowing the real reason for his estrangement from the magazine, which was the notorious Cecil Parkinson story of 1985, described in Chapter Two.

There is no need to go into that story further than to say that the splendid splash story that the *Mail* won by floating the story of Parkinson's latest affair in the *Eye* and then reporting the resulting furore, although free of legal risk, created problems for *Mail* editor Sir David English.

He had his own private contacts in the Tory party, and his 1982 knighthood for services to journalism was seen by some to have been a reward for his staunch support for Margaret Thatcher. The Prime Minister had a high regard for Parkinson, and tried hard to keep him in the Cabinet long after the Sara Keays affair had become unmanageable. English was also on friendly terms with Parkinson and during the course of the *Daily Mail*'s inquiries into the story Parkinson had assured him that there was not a shred of truth in the gossip.

Sir David was happy with that assurance, and the *Daily Mail*'s inquiries were dropped. When it surfaced in *Private Eye*, Parkinson was not unjustified in suspecting that the

Mail was involved. It was known that Dempster was an *Eye* contributor – he had taken no trouble to conceal it – so it would have been natural for Parkinson to believe that the *Eye* story emanated from the *Mail* offices.

Sir David English has been a successful editor of the *Daily Mail* since 1971. The rival *Daily Express* has, in its attempts to match his flair, got through no fewer than seven editors in that time. He is also a major figure in the business hierarchy of the large Associated Newspapers Group. He moves in a rarefied political stratosphere where it would have been considered most unseemly to be connected with a *Private Eye* attack on Parkinson.

Happily for him, the suspicion was never raised. Dempster gave an interview to a *Sunday Times* reporter suggesting that the story had originated in the *Eye* itself. He had been asked by people at the *Eye* to confirm the story, he said, and he had told them he knew nothing to support such an idea. Sir David English had to weigh this statement against the next issue of the *Eye*, in which Ingrams – writing in a 'Gnome' leader – named Dempster as the author of the *Eye* story.

It was this episode that prompted Dempster to accuse the *Eye* of nearly losing him his job at the *Mail*. But as we have seen, his attempts to blame Hislop for failing to check his Parkinson story did not impress Ingrams. Dempster insisted that the sacking of Hislop was the price of his return to the *Eye*. But Hislop was not fired, and Dempster has not returned.

An odd episode took place on the day Ingrams announced that he was standing down in favour of Hislop. Dempster appeared outside the *Eye*'s front window in Carlisle Street and waved at the staff in high good humour. He came in, congratulated Ingrams, and insisted on driving his new enemy to Paddington in the large, white BMW provided for him by the *Daily Mail*. He could not have been friendlier, which was odd since Ingrams had now actually *promoted* the hated Hislop.

Dempster can perhaps be faulted in the Parkinson affair;

but Ingrams could have retrieved the situation with a compromise if he had so wanted. Dempster demanded the sacking of Hislop, I am convinced, because that would have made it easier for him to rationalise in his mind what he saw as his own honourable role in the affair. But Ingrams preferred to support Hislop outright. Hislop had printed the Parkinson story after being warned by the duty lawyer on press day that it was likely to attract legal action. He had also spoken to Dempster, although there is dispute as to what was actually said. What is not in dispute is that Hislop knew the *Eye* was taking a chance in publishing the story. Even if Dempster had said the story was 'copper bottomed' – a favourite term of eager *Eye* contributors – Hislop had the warning of the lawyer, as well as of his own common sense. It was not as if he *had* to put it in – there is always something lying around that can be stuck in at the last moment.

Dempster, on the other hand, was wrong to deny his involvement to *The Sunday Times* for if the *Eye* had had a defence of the item, Dempster's recantation destroyed it. How could *Private Eye* have gone into court with any kind of defence after the 'Grovel' column's chief contributor had said publicly that the item was untrue. But by then Dempster was under severe pressure from Sir David English to put as much distance between himself and the story as possible. The row also introduced a new element of personal responsibility into *Eye* politics. There had been many rows in the past following 'Grovel' stories, but rarely was Dempster asked to take personal responsibility for his stories. Ingrams was usually happy to answer press questions about the provenance of 'Grovel' items, but in his absence it was Dempster who was 'fingered', rather than Hislop as stand-in editor. If Ingrams had been there, would *The Sunday Times* have built their story around the interview with Dempster? It is unlikely. Ingrams is 'Lord Gnome', the recognised authority on all matters pertaining to the *Eye*. He would have handled the affair, leaving Dempster free to help in any way he could with the *Eye*'s defence. But these were changing times at *Private Eye*. Hislop was being groomed for succession, and he had to be protected. Dempster had become another 'Yesterday's Man'. He could be thrown to the wolves.

Ingrams afterwards defended himself by saying that Dempster had gone mad – had let fame go to his head. He had given up publishing interesting, contentious information about the eminent and was now sucking up to famous people. He, like his targets of yesteryear, had now to be attacked. And so Dempster became a stock joke character in the funny pages. I remarked once that Dempster resembled an old tiger who just wanted to sit happily in a gilded cage, 'grooming' his brilliantly-plumed new friends. *Private Eye* rattled the bars now and then, disturbing their tranquillity. Ingrams was pleased with the analogy. 'Rattle that cage!' he would cry whenever Dempster's name was mentioned.

In April 1986, Ingrams wrote a short account of Dempster's role in the Parkinson affair for issue 634:

> In March 1985 Dumpster, well known to be 'Grovel', partly as a result of his own boasting in the Press and on TV, submitted an item linking Cecil Parkinson, then recovering from the effects of the Sara Keays affair, with another secretary. It was printed in *Eye* 606.
>
> Tipped off by a *Daily Mail* hack, who in turn had been alerted by Dumpster, that the item was about to appear, Parkinson successfully applied to the High Court for an injunction stopping publication of the *Eye*. As a result all copies of issue 606 were withdrawn.
>
> The following Sunday Dumpster, who had previously given the *Eye* vague assurances of help, was quoted in *The Sunday Times* denying that he had written the article.
>
> He added: 'I saw the story before it went in and said I knew nothing that could substantiate it in court.'
>
> This Double Lie ensured that the *Eye* had no defence in any subsequent litigation brought by Parkinson.

Dempster invited Auberon Waugh to luncheon at the Connaught Hotel to discuss the situation. Waugh said afterwards that his host's mercurial temperament was even more vividly on display than usual. Dempster promised dire revenge on his tormentors, and wallowed in what Waugh called 'babyish self pity'. Waugh counselled Ingrams in a telephone call after the lunch: 'Go easy on the old boy, he's in a bad way.'

Dempster was a great loss to the *Eye*. Although most of his stories went into 'Grovel', he was always ready to assist on other leads that required his special knowledge of the rich and powerful – especially those facts about them that had not been widely publicised. It was he who had brought to the *Eye* the story that was to result in their most protracted and costly saga – the Jimmy Goldsmith affair, described in Chapter Four.

Ingrams has said that the Goldsmith affair was good for *Private Eye*. He concludes *Goldenballs* by saying: '. . . it is likely that the extraordinary amount of publicity generated by the case more than helped to restore the circulation that we lost'. There is little doubt that in his years at the *Eye* Dempster also helped to win the magazine new readers. He poured into the 'Grovel' column all the energy and enthusiasm and element of danger that was the chief attraction of his *Daily Mail* column in its earlier days.

But Dempster and Ingrams were never close friends – their natures are very different. Dempster always treated Ingrams with great deference. While he unashamedly pursued material wealth and social position, Ingrams appeared to covet neither. Dempster wore expensively-made suits, Turnbull and Asser shirts and Gucci shoes, while Ingrams stuck to his faded corduroy, Marks and Spencer cotton shirts and mis-shapen walking shoes. They made a delightfully odd pair, chuckling at the corner table upstairs in the Gay Hussar.

In some ways their relationship reminded me of the one between the powerful gossip columnist played by Burt Lancaster in *The Sweet Smell of Success* and the eager-to-please public relations man played by Tony Curtis. Dempster, playing the Tony Curtis role, would come to see Ingrams, playing the Burt Lancaster role, with the latest items he considered worthy of publication. Ingrams was never rude or overbearing to Dempster. His way of dealing with this richly-plumed creature was almost ducal: he listened with pleasure to all the outrageous stories, but was always firm about what he wanted from Dempster – and Dempster always did his best to comply.

On our way out of the Gay Hussar we often had to walk through the ground-floor section of the restaurant which, as often as not, would have a sprinkling of Dempster and *Private Eye* victims among its patrons. Both Dempster and Ingrams seemed to take pleasure in being seen in each other's company, as if believing that the sight of them together might discourage their enemies.

Waugh's own feud with Ingrams was more subtle. On a personal level he complained about what he saw as the editor's increasing puritanism – his dislike of drinking and drinkers, together with his revulsion for sex. Ingrams was now more strict about the 'massage' small ads, saying, only partly in jest, that he wanted to clear the 'filth' out of these pages. Waugh, like *Private Eye*'s principal shareholder Peter Cook, is an enthusiast of massage parlours, both at home and in Thailand.

But it was Ingrams' conservatism in another area that angered Waugh more. Towards the end of his reign, the editor was no longer prepared to fight libel cases. Like his father, Evelyn Waugh, Bron likes to concentrate his attacks on a small collection of subjects that particularly incense him. The modern attitude to libel is one of them. In general, Waugh, like Ingrams, believes that few eminent people are really damaged by what is said about them in the papers; they are persuaded to sue by lawyers who stand to gain by the proceedings and also by the knowledge that such damages as they might obtain are tax-free.

Of course, there is a risk that they might lose, in which case they will probably have to pay heavy costs. But what if they are supported in their action by their employers? Then their risk is minimised: on the one hand they may win a large sum in recompense for a slighting story about them; on the other hand, if they lose, their employers will pick up the bill anyway. Going to law, especially in libel cases, is very much like gambling. There are a certain imponderables that must be weighed up: the weight of the legal arguments for and against a case; the composition of the jury on the day; the attitude of the judge; and, if the litigants are famous, whether the climate of opinion is behind them at the time of the trial. A litigant and his or her lawyers will balance these considerations, work out the odds, then decide whether to sue or not. The question as to whether a litigant's career and financial prospects are really jeopardised by the original article hardly comes into it.

In 1983 Waugh received at *Private Eye* a letter on *Sunday Times* notepaper purporting to be from Claire Tomalin, then the paper's literary editor. Enclosed was a selection of *Lesbian and Gay Fiction*, edited by Adam Mars-Jones. The letter asked for a 600-word review. It ended: 'Before starting please phone me to let me know what sort of review you are going to write. I understand you are sympathetic to the gay movement and I would expect a generous piece.'

Waugh should have known it was a joke. No one in journalism, far less in literary journalism, could have believed that he was a supporter of homosexuals, whom he insists on calling 'homosexualists'. His most famous intervention in public affairs had been his attendance at the Jeremy Thorpe trial, his subsequent book about the affair, and his standing against Thorpe at a by-election as the candidate for the 'Dog Lover's Party'. In addition, what he sees as the pretensions of those who review books in the Sunday newspapers has long been a favourite target. It is unlikely that a literary editor will ever seek to influence the opinions of any of their reviewers, particularly those of Auberon Waugh. But instead of consigning the letter to the waste-paper basket, or ringing Ms Tomalin to confirm that she had not sent it, he put a jokey item in his *Eye* diary rebuking her for seeking to bias reviewers. This ended with the line: 'It makes me wonder about all those crazy

Somerset majors who say there is a left-wing, homosexual conspiracy in the media.'

Ms Tomalin put the matter in the hands of the *Sunday Times* legal department, and on the Tuesday after his diary item appeared a writ for libel arrived, accompanied by a letter demanding an apology, a retraction, and damages for what the *Sunday Times* solicitors called 'as gross, baseless and hurtful a libel as it is possible to imagine'.

Waugh printed a retraction and an apology he had composed himself in his next diary. Ingrams agreed to fight the case if this did not do the trick. Waugh believed that no British jury or judge would award Ms Tomalin more than five pence in damages, and he was looking forward to his day in court. Ingrams was also enthusiastic. Waugh later described him as 'full of robust enthusiasm – charming, witty and bold . . .'

In the event, *Private Eye* did not fight the case. A prior action brought by an obscure Welsh solicitor had gone against them. Damages were paid, as well as costs amounting to in excess of £100,000. Ingrams, fearing the prospect of the Tomalin case dragging on for months, with similarly expensive consequences for the *Eye*, decided to settle, and paid Ms Tomalin £2,000.

This infuriated Waugh. He wrote a series of articles deploring the settlement. In one he said: 'It seems to me that if one loses one's faith in the ultimate common sense of the courts one might as well become a crook or a politician. Poor Ingrams, I feel he may be dying or going mad.' The argument that the case could have cost tens of thousands of pounds cut no ice with him. *Private Eye*, he felt, had a duty to fight what he saw as an abuse of the legal system.

Waugh's argument highlights an interesting aspect of *Private Eye*'s *raison d'être*. While it might seem prudent and sensible for a conventional publication to avoid libel cases, that cannot be true of *Private Eye*. As Judge Skinner remarked, it is a 'high risk' publication. That is why it exists. If it is no longer prepared to take risks, it cannot justifiably claim to be a serious publication.

Waugh was not one of the original *Private Eye* team, but his columns, begun as a lampoon of the Alan Brien diary in *The Sunday Times*, were considered one of the chief attractions of the magazine. A collection of them, *The Diaries of Auberon Waugh: A Turbulent Decade, 1976 to 1985*, published by *Private Eye* and André Deutsch, sold well. Certainly the author was not bashful about self-publicity, and contrived to mention his book in many of the articles he wrote in other magazines around publication day. *Spectator* readers were urged: 'It is so cheap, the best thing might be to buy a couple of dozen and give them to all your friends at Christmas.'

Like Ingrams, he is a formidably funny man. His diary was a unique synthesis of fact and fantasy which illuminated his targets brilliantly. His technique was to describe his targets exactly as he saw them and then, with an effortless sleight of hand that made it difficult to judge where the facts ended and the fun began, he would draw his hapless victims into an absurd world of his own invention. A straightforward factual description of behaviour can be wildly funny, as the court reports in the *Daily Telegraph* often were. Waugh took the process a stage further in *Private Eye*. Some of his items were cruel, especially those he composed about individuals who had sued the *Eye*, but his diary was seldom less that hilarious.

Waugh lovingly rotated his attacks upon a wide-ranging demonology of people in the aristocracy, journalism and politics. When *Observer* journalist Nora Beloff married, at a late age, her colleague Clifford Makins, the occasion did not go unremarked in Waugh's diary. As she had sued both Waugh and *Private Eye*, perhaps Miss Beloff should have expected attack. But even the sophisticated mind of a senior political correspondent like herself could not have imagined what Waugh had in store for her on 4 March 1977:

I had hoped to be asked to be best man at Nora Beloff's wedding today, since I imagine it was I who supplied a large part of the bride's dowry. It makes me happy to think that the £3,000 I gave her in libel damages a few years ago might have helped her find such a suitable husband as Clifford Makins, the well-known journalist.

Perhaps I had better explain myself. Like Nora, I had been a political correspondent for years when, tantalised by the un-availability of my opposite number on the *Observer*, I decided to make a joke about her. As it turned out, whether from in-competence or over-excitement, I made an allegation about her personal life of such a foul and loathsome nature that even now I blush to the roots of my remaining hair when I think about it.

For 56 long summers, Nora had resisted the advances of the coarser sex. Nothing will be the same again. Even as I write, I imagine that Clifford Makins is exploring the unimaginable delights of her body, never sweeter than when first sampled.

The note concluded with the wedding night advice to Makins that he should treat his new bride like a motor:

Keep her steady on the straight, watch out for warning lights on the ignition and lubrication dials and when you reckon she's run in, give her all you've got.

Waugh has never been against anything apart from bad people. Issues of any kind he sees simply as the means by which immature, potty-trained, power-mad zealots seek to corral and harness the will of idle, stupid people. When pronouncing his enthusiasm for a certain cause – such as the claims of Peregrine Worsthorne to a knighthood – he is more likely to be teasing than declaring his sympathies. His ostensible support of the battery system of rearing chickens, because he makes the methods sound so uniquely horrible, must have been designed to bait animal rightists as much as to press home the case for battery farming:

In the Co-operative Agricole de Lauragais, to which I belong, the battery system has been refined. We have developed the featherless chicken, which saves the labour of plucking it. It lays shell-less eggs contained in the membraneous tissue, slightly reminiscent of plastic. Many modern housewives go mad at the extra effort involved in breaking eggs. These birds are unable to stand up, which is sensible because they have nowhere to go.

Waugh wrote his diary in longhand, and sat by the type-setter to supervise its transference onto the page. He was popular with all the *Eye* staff because of his cheery humour. The arrival of this balding, tubby figure attired in his father's tweed coat, the fogeyish ensemble often completed by a rakishly-worn fedora, was always an event at *Private Eye*. He wore his father's old suits, too, suspended by red braces, and smoked cigarettes incessantly.

If his column was 'over' he would cut it down to size. When he was finished, Ingrams would be summoned to look it over before it was pasted into Tony Rushton's pages. Ingrams rarely altered a word.

Ingrams' humour always worked best in co-operation with others – he was not only amusing himself, but a cause of wit in others. His own writing was simple, clear and funny, but it lacked Waugh's soaring flights of fantasy. In a sense, Waugh's column – like all great diary columns – was a paper within a paper. Waugh is dismissive about other parts of *Private Eye*, particularly 'straight' journalism such as the Penny Junor column. He is also scornful of Paul Foot's 'crybaby' stories about evil politicians and businessmen who deceive the public, his view being that anyone who puts his trust in such people in the first place, like General George Custer, has got it coming.

However, he managed to share a tiny office at the Greek Street offices with both Foot and Michael Gillard, the some-what doleful author of the 'In the City' column. Often peals of laughter could be heard from this odd trio. Waugh used to toss his cigarettes out of the window, and on one occasion an angry bag lady ascended the stairs to claim that he had set fire to her hair.

He was never paid more than £238 for each of his *Eye* articles – considerably less than his reward for less amusing stuff in national newspapers and magazines. *Private Eye* was his principal roost, although he contributed a weekly

1200-word essay to the *Spectator*. Occasionally this was no more than a longer version of something he had said more pithily in the *Eye*. Waugh also generated a certain quantity of ideas each week and spread them skilfully around several outlets. He had been sacked from *The Times* for suggesting lightheartedly that Muslims wore baggy trousers because they believed that Allah would be reborn to a man – an article which resulted in the burning down of the British Library in Rawalpindi. Thereafter, he resolved to retain several outlets so that fear of giving offence would not jeopardise the quality of his output.

At *Private Eye* Waugh had no qualms about biting the hand that fed him. Occasionally he would make oblique jokes about 'Ingram', and he portrayed 'Lord Gnome' in his diary as a mad, Howard Hughes-type figure surrounded by nurses. If Ingrams took offence he took care not to show it. But the Waugh family friendship with the Ingrams family did not always prosper. Mary considered Bron disloyal, and was particularly incensed about his speech at the farewell lunch given for him by Ingrams. She snapped that Hislop's installation had nothing to do with Waugh, which was perfectly true, 'because he has left now'. He was a servant who had given good service in his time but had now left, and it was impudent of him to venture opinions about the new staffing arrangements.

Waugh's other main source of income was Sir David English's *Daily Mail* – for some reason he always put English's name in quotes, as if to suggest that it had been made up. He also wrote for the *Sunday Telegraph*, where the deputy editor – in 1986 he became editor – was Peregrine Worsthorne. Waugh made regular pleas in his column on Worsthorne's behalf, saying that the commentator should be knighted and comparing Perry's plight with that of P. J. Wodehouse before he was finally knighted in his nineties. This was known to infuriate Worsthorne, perhaps because Waugh's support in this matter was hardly likely to be helpful. Of course, it delighted Ingrams, although he himself was notably more cautious about offending those outside the *Eye* who occasionally sought his services.

Waugh is a brave man in ways that are not widely known about. He was badly injured during his National Service when a jammed machine-gun he was trying to fix to an army patrol car began firing, and from time to time he has to be admitted to hospital to have fluids drained from the chasms this has left in his chest. Despite his professed hatred of the working classes, he usually chooses to admit himself to a public ward, where he takes part in and greatly enjoys the badinage.

I remember visiting him once with Ingrams – the occasion provided a perfect example of the truism about visitors going to hospital to be cheered up by the patients. Waugh, although weak and in pain, was in great form, while Ingrams sat with a doleful countenance. He did not actually eat Waugh's grapes, but in most other respects he was the type of visitor a hospital patient needs like a lumbar puncture.

Waugh is a far more adventurous man than Ingrams, who frequently did not even possess an up-to-date passport. Ingrams has sallied forth cautiously on staid foreign trips – A. J. P. Taylor took him to Venice, and he later became attached to Malta. But Waugh travels frequently, immersing himself, for instance, in the nightlife of Bangkok, and riding for miles at night on the back of a motorbike to sample a few pipes of opium.

Ingrams is a brave man, too, but his strengths are internal. He is much more bound up in himself than Waugh and, partly because he does not drink, he is not partial to social occasions. He defends himself by saying that such gatherings are full of 'bores', and that people who are drinking do not realise when they are becoming loud and boring. This is true enough as far as it goes; but Ingrams does not seem to appreciate that his own aloofness, his silences and his brooding are also boring to others. Waugh is rarely boring – drunk or sober. He also shows a generosity rare in writers by being willing to share his jokes with others.

In the 1980s Waugh's appearances at the fortnightly

luncheon became irregular, then he dropped off the guest list altogether. Polite as ever, he explained this away by saying he had less time, which was true but not the whole story. In fact he had little time for the kind of people who were appearing at *Eye* luncheons – especially those there to grind their own political axe.

Waugh's preference was for a guest list comprising mainly amusing and/or famous people who, by their gossip, would inspire the *Eye* each fortnight to select a new raft of targets for its satire, jokes and 'Grovel' column. But, partly for practical reasons, Ingrams had surrendered power over the guest list to hacks on the magazine, who self-servingly sought to invite people who could be expected to furnish 'hard' information for the news and business sections, as well as give them jobs.

In this respect, Waugh's attendance at the lunches was often counter-productive in that he tended to tease those who came to provide damaging information about their rivals. But he was also capable of inspiring conversations that were revealing. I remember one hilarious inquiry conducted into the life and work of the late Lord Mountbatten, in which Waugh was joined by the Tory MP Alan Clark. Clark, a right-winger, said he had always suspected Mountbatten of having been, if not a Soviet agent, a sympathiser of the Moscow regime. He claimed that Mountbatten had worked behind the scenes to stop Britain getting American Polaris nuclear missiles. Waugh's gift on these occasions was his refusal to be surprised by anything he heard, which of course had the effect of encouraging storytellers to go to even greater lengths in providing verisimilitude. Since he was also very amusing company, important people who could be valuable to the *Eye* were keen to attend the lunches.

The lunches were far less amusing and stimulating when he ceased to attend. That was true also of Dempster, who had dropped out of them years before for much the same reasons as Waugh.

Like Dempster before him, Waugh left *Private Eye* partly

because he felt that Ingrams had let him down. Dempster believed he had come close to losing his job on the *Daily Mail* because of the *Eye*'s part in the Parkinson affair – and yet Ingrams had been unsympathetic. The editor had promised Waugh that he would fight the Tomalin case – and yet while Waugh was away he changed his mind and settled. 'He ratted, that's the point,' Waugh told me without bitterness.

There might also have been some friction especially on the part of Mary Ingrams over Waugh's continuing friendship with another *Eye* 'Yesterday's Man', Patrick Marnham.

Marnham had finally severed his ties after publication of *The Private Eye Story* in 1982.

This semi-official history of *Private Eye* had been Ingrams' idea to commemorate the magazine's twenty-first anniversary. The *Eye* has always shrewdly exploited such occasions – an earlier burst of publicity had attended the arrival of the 500th issue. Marnham is an excellent writer, and he had contributed to the *Eye* on and off since 1966.

He had written a number of previous books, but the one that most took Ingrams' fancy was *Lourdes: A Modern Pilgrimage*, which set out to provide a serious account of the French religious shrine. Marnham told me at the time: 'He thought the Lourdes book was brilliant and gave it a rave review somewhere.' What did he like about it? 'Oh, I think he singled out the brilliant writing. I think he was particularly impressed by the descriptive passages.'

Marnham is the son of the royal surgeon Sir Ralph Marnham, and he was educated at the Roman Catholic public school Downside. Later he was to become a fierce critic of Cardinal Hume, Archbishop of Westminster. He started the *Eye*'s 'Grovel' column, and set a fantastical Waugh-like tone to it that unfortunately did not survive his departure.

Over the years he had quarrelled often with Ingrams, but they always managed to patch things up. Ingrams once voiced this opinion of the acclaimed author of *The Private*

Eye Story; 'Everyone quite likes Marnham, but few become friends of his.'

Like Ingrams he is an indolent man, who in his *Eye* days wore scruffy sports jackets, torn shirts and blue jeans. His hair is often long and unkempt and, again like Ingrams, his sallow, handsome face is pitted with acne scars. He has a delightfully mischievous sense of humour, and is a scholar in the Waugh rather than Ingrams school of *Eye* thought: the joke, the tease, was the thing; heavy, boring *Eye* campaigns had no appeal for him.

In the introduction to *The Private Eye Story* he describes his discovery of *Private Eye* thus:

> One gloomy afternoon in March I was sitting in the library of Gray's Inn pretending to prepare for the Bar finals when my friend, David Dodd, later a lecturer in criminology at Georgetown University, Guyana, wandered in with a copy of the latest issue . . . The future lecturer pointed out an advertisement for 'editorial assistant, preferably graduate, with knowledge of politics and journalism' which he suggested I should answer . . . By the time the exam results came through, it was too late. I had escaped from the laws of England disguised as a journalist, an occupation which in those informal days required no more than a mild display of aptitude and interest.

Marnham was teased at the *Eye* for his pro-Arab stance, but he liked to point out that he was born in Jerusalem and that he subscribed to the *Jewish Chronicle*. He once told me proudly that as a teenager he had won Murren's downhill 'roped pairs' skiing race the Scaramanga and that his partner was one Peter Rosenberg – 'and he was Jewish'.

However, he did not subscribe to the *Jewish Chronicle* wholly out of a benign interest in the Jewish community. He took a particular interest in the doings of prominent Jewish businessmen, especially those who had become close to the Prime Minister at the time, Harold Wilson. He was Ingrams' choice to write up the Sir James Goldsmith story in *Private Eye* which, apart from the financier himself, eventually involved Goldsmith's Jewish lawyer into the bargain.

At the *Eye* his views on the Middle East were occasionally problematical. One of the many rows about the early draft of the book concerned the long-time *Eye* contributor Barry Fantoni. The disagreement was resolved, but Marnham said in an interview after publication: 'Fantoni said I had portrayed him as a Jewish sex maniac and half-wit. So I put in other aspects of his life there. Now he is even angrier.'

It has to be said that it was an enormously pompous decision of Ingrams to commission an official history of the *Eye*; and it might have been anticipated – given Marnham's independent nature – that the book would cause trouble. Cash said that Marnham had been encouraged to do the book independently of the *Eye*, and that he should have done so. On the other hand, the idea had been *Private Eye*'s, and Marnham was dependent on them to help with the research. He received an advance of £15,000 and the book was a bestseller – but not before it had caused his final estrangement from his former colleagues. As in the other rows, the two sides cannot agree on the reasons for the dispute, except to say that Ingrams disapproved of parts of Marnham's book. He thought that it dwelt too long on the news and gossip side of the *Eye* and neglected the jokes and lampoons.

Ingrams was furious about the first draft, demanded that parts of it be rewritten, and undertook to write some of them himself. In the end everyone concerned – except the readers – were depressed about the book. Marnham enraged Ingrams further by declining to take part in a nationwide publicity tour that had been arranged. Despite his aloofness, Ingrams is a determined self-publicist who would have been prepared to sign books in the Orkneys; on the other hand, Marnham has a secretive, reclusive personality, which is not rare among journalists who have specialised in writing about controversial subjects.

Ingrams recognised that it had been unwise to ask Marnham to do the book; and he accused Marnham of humbug for accepting a large amount of money to write the story and then virtually disowning it after publication.

The end result was that Marnham became a 'Yesterday's Man', mentioned by Ingrams, if at all, with that sorrowful disdain he reserves for those of his flock – Dempster, Waugh, and others – who have become mad, bad or immoral.

Despite his laziness, Marnham was a loss to *Private Eye*. Sophisticated and amusing, he had an eye for stories that were important, and a sparkling wit that had made his 'Grovel' column a delightful tease – in contrast to the sledgehammer technique of his successor, Nigel Dempster.

The Private Eye Story read oddly to anyone who worked at the *Eye* at the time the book was published. Marnham put a distance between himself and his *Eye* colleagues, and gave prominence to the idea that *Private Eye* had been corrupted by the values of Fleet Street by putting this and similar sentiments into the mouths of John Wells and Christopher Booker – two pranksters who were happy to moonlight in the *Eye* gutter part-time, but were anxious to assure the upper-class people they cultivated that they deplored the magazine's more egregious content.

In a sense, Patrick Marnham wrote himself out of *Private Eye* by taking on the book. But he was eager to take part in the fracas over Hislop's appointment, and said he would contribute again if neither Ingrams nor Hislop was in control of what he wrote.

Marnham's book is very useful in gaining an understanding of how *Private Eye* started, and he is occasionally sharp in his observations about Ingrams. His final chapter was entitled 'A Faint Holiness':

Holiness or not, he has a captivating charm, since the severest critics among his old friends will always respond to his re-proffered friendship after a bitter disagreement. His greatest quality as an editor is his judgement. This is something that has grown with the job. Again and again when the paper has been faced with the most appalling legal threats, Ingrams has charted the course ahead, taking advice as it suited him but analysing the risks largely by himself and usually very accurately. He also stands solidly behind his contributors. His most baffling weakness is his reluctance to give credit to the work of others.

Ingrams had re-proffered friendship to Marnham several times after past rows. But once the book was published it was all over.

Marnham's exit line, characteristically understated, was contained in the introduction to *The Private Eye Story*. He reminded readers of his 'sixteen contented years' as an anonymous contributor, and he said the position should have given him an advantage in writing an 'authorised history from a detached point of view'. However:

> I find, having finished the book, which I was invited to write by Richard Ingrams, and which is published by André Deutsch and Private Eye jointly, that my account is sufficiently detached to have evoked strong and critical disagreement from some of those who founded the paper.

Marnham's departure was certainly more decorous, on the surface at least, than that of his colleague Martin Tomkinson, who left suddenly in 1981 after nearly ten years. The tall, bearded Tomkinson joined Virgin boss Richard Branson's new *Event* listings magazine after leaving the *Eye* abruptly on the eve of its twentieth anniversary. His departure followed a disagreement between him, Ingrams and Cash about payments made to individuals whom Tomkinson said were his informants; but Tomkinson was also a drinker, and had occasionally irritated Ingrams by frequenting afternoon clubs in Soho.

Event ripped into *Private Eye*, saying that Fleet Street journalists on its staff – Dempster, Foot, myself and Tomkinson, who was paid a retainer by the *Daily Mirror* – had conspired to keep out a story about the marital problems of a *Mirror* executive. Allegedly neglected by her husband, who was said to be attentive to *Mirror* secretaries, she had indulged in a 'one night stand' with one of his junior colleagues. This man had been forced to leave the *Mirror* as a result.

There was a germ of truth in the allegations, in that Paul Foot had asked Ingrams not to run the story. But Ingrams had replied that he wasn't thinking of putting it in anyway, 'as it was just about a bunch of boring *Mirror* hacks getting their legs over'. Branson, whom the *Eye* described regularly as 'a reptilian little shit', built a general attack on the *Eye* and the *Mirror* over three issues of *Event*. The fourth instalment, however, took the form of a full-page retraction and apology to the *Mirror*.

Branson had taken care to arrange a figleaf of protection for his principal source of information, Martin Tomkinson, by adding the name of Tomkinson to the roll-call of shame. There was something of a witch-hunt among *Eye* men to find the culprit, but Tomkinson was not suspected because he was still on the *Eye*, and because of Branson's ruse. What most of us did not know was that Tomkinson was on the brink of resignation after several sessions with Ingrams and Cash about the payments-to-contributors controversy – and that did not come out at the time.

Tomkinson is a beefy former student of the London School of Economics who contributed mainly to the 'Business News' pages. He was not a skilled news writer like Foot and Gillard, with whom he worked, but his political animus against rich businessmen compensated to some degree for that shortcoming. Having had a state education, he was often, especially after lunch, derisive about the public-school atmosphere at *Private Eye*. He called Ingrams 'Dick'; Ingrams called him 'Tombo' and 'Matey'.

Over his years at the *Eye* Tomkinson appeared to grow cynical about his once-strong socialist convictions. He did not earn much from the *Eye*, and was expected to supplement his income from work elsewhere. This made life difficult for him, especially after the birth of his child. He was introduced by fellow *Eye* contributor Jeffrey 'Colonel Mad'

Bernard to wealthy, controversial men such as Playboy boss Victor Lownes and racehorse owner Charles St George. Both were free with their hospitality. The latter gave Tomkinson the keys to his Mercedes Benz one night after a party and said he could return it when he felt like it. St George later helped Tomkinson with the mortgage on a small house in Hackney, north London. It was never clear what Lownes or St George expected from Tomkinson in return. Certainly there was no evidence that he had suppressed interesting details about them that could have gone into the *Eye*.

He had played for the *Private Eye* cricket team, and enjoyed the type of friendship with Ingrams that the editor reserves for people who are useful to him. He also introduced Paul Halloran to the *Eye*, and Halloran took his job in the end. He became a 'Yesterday's Man', whose photograph, like Marnham's, adorns the front wall of the *Eye* offices. The picture shows Tomkinson with Ingrams and Bernard strolling along Greek Street. All of them are laughing merrily. When he – and Bernard – had gone, a bubble appeared above Tomkinson's head which had him saying to Bernard: 'He says we've been fired.'

'Tombo' was occasionally seen afterwards in the Coach and Horses, where he would be ignored by Ingrams. From time to time a member of staff would come in with news that Tomkinson was not doing well as a freelance journalist. But there was no question of him ever being re-hired. He had served his purpose, blotted his copybook, and was out.

Bernard's love affair with Ingrams was of a much shorter duration. He had become a famous figure in racing circles, having written for *The Sporting Life*, and in Soho, where he did most of his heaving drinking. It is said that he was fired from *The Sporting Life* after being sick during the course of a speech at a black tie dinner.

Ingrams took up Bernard enthusiastically in 1977, engaging him to write a defamatory column about racing types under the pseudonym 'Colonel Mad'. The column concentrated on the off-course behaviour of trainers and jockeys, with particular emphasis on drinking, gambling and womanising ('leg-overs' in *Eye* parlance). Like the early 'Grovel' and Waugh's diary, Bernard avoided litigation by the use of absurd exaggeration.

He is a formidable drinker, and his habits have wrecked his liver and pancreas. On at least two occasions while he was doing the column he had to be taken to hospital. Ingrams tried to persuade Bernard to stop drinking, and was furious when on one occasion he discovered that 'Colonel Mad' was being supplied with vodka by friends while lying seriously ill in a ward at the Radcliffe Infirmary, Oxford.

In the end Ingrams killed 'Colonel Mad', to Bernard's bitter disappointment. Bernard had put great efforts into the column, and believed that it had increased sales of the *Eye*. But Ingrams said: 'He'll never pull himself together if we keep subsidising his drinking.'

Bernard is a handful, but he is also a witty and gifted writer, and there is no question that he has a following. He was taken up subsequently by Alexander Chancellor at the *Spectator* who capitalised on Bernard's louche habits by getting him to write about them weekly under the title 'Low Life'. This is literally a column about a man drinking himself to death. While Ingrams deplored Bernard's habits, and refused to subsidise them, Chancellor – himself a drinker – made the best of his contributor, so that his column has become a kind of mascot for boozers.

Bernard continued to drink at the Coach and Horses, a yard from the *Eye* table, after he was fired. He got over the sacking, especially when the *Spectator* provided him with a new platform, and would often seek to engage Ingrams in friendly conversation; but he usually got the glazed eyes treatment. However, Ingrams' daughter Jubby is friendly with Bernard, and on at least one occasion they have enjoyed a night on the town together.

Bernard's drinking friends at the Coach include Richard West, another old *Eye* stalwart who has been frozen out. West is a brilliant journalist whom many consider to have produced some of the best reporting from the Vietnam War. He began to contribute to *Private Eye* in around 1965. He wrote hundreds of stories for the magazine, and was involved in the epic Goldsmith litigation. West is married to the Irish-born journalist Mary Kenny. Twenty years after he first began writing for *Private Eye*, Ingrams will scarcely speak to him any more. West has always been a drinker, but is also now a 'bore'. If he has any stories he has to filter them through the brusque Halloran who, sensing Ingrams' approval, is inclined to dismiss them as 'balls', and West as an old soak. West drinks with Bernard a yard from the table at which Ingrams sits with his new protégés. He is always ignored. On every second Wednesday, if West and Bernard are in the Coach, those invited to the luncheon that day will pass them on their way up the stairs. I have occasionally asked Ingrams about West, whom I like and respect.

He looks sorrowful and says that the trouble with Dick is that he drinks and is careless with facts. Ingrams' mentor, Claud Cockburn, also liked to drink, and was careless about facts on a grand scale. Ingrams accepts the inconsistency without rancour, but he has never elaborated on the freezing out of Dick West.

West, Tomkinson and Bernard all served a purpose at various times, but Ingrams has proved to be no different from any other employer when a face does not fit any more. Their contributions had all been anonymous or, in the case of Bernard, pseudonymous. When it was time for them to go the shortcomings that had been tolerated while they were fruitful contributors were given as the reasons for their departure.

Keith Raffan is a rare exception to this rule. He used the *Eye* brilliantly, and when Ingrams was useful to him no longer he dumped Lord Gnome without ceremony. Afterwards, in 1983, he entered the House of Commons as the Tory member for the Welsh seat of Delwyn. His entry in *Who's Who*, unlike Nigel Dempster's, makes no mention of his *Eye* years, nor of his role on the gossip column in the *Sunday*

Express presided over by Lady Olga Maitland. But he does concede that he was 'Parly Correspondent, *Daily Express*, 1981–83'.

Nothing Raffan ever wrote for the *Daily Express* about parliament, or anything else, was as spicy as the material he sent in to his *Eye* column, 'HP Sauce' by Backbiter. He launched a series called 'The New Boys', a vitriolic summary of the achievements, or otherwise, of fledgling members of the Commons. A constant and admirable theme of the column was the crazed ambition of some new MPs for position and status. Raffan had contested two seats for the Tories in 1974 – Dulwich and East Aberdeenshire – and everything he learned about the struggles of young politicians on the make informed his bitter vignettes in *Private Eye*.

Raffan is a slimly-built, excitable young bachelor, who made his mark early when, as chairman of a Tory pressure group, he turned Edward Heath's famous remark about Lonrho boss Rowland 'Tiny' Rowlands being the 'unacceptable face of capitalism' back on its author, calling the former Tory Prime Minister 'the unacceptable face of conservatism'. Ingrams liked Raffan's sparkling, bitchy copy, but did not care greatly for its author. Raffan was paid £70 an issue for 'HP Sauce', but he did it for love rather than money.

He left the *Eye* before the 1983 election, and never communicated directly with his former colleagues again. But he ought to have known that the *Eye*, like the Mafia, is not an easy organisation to forget. Shortly after he was elected, he himself became the subject of a bitchy 'New Boy' piece, and the *Guardian* diary unhelpfully pointed out that he had once been the column's author.

Raffan is a good example of how the *Eye* can be useful to a rising young politician who feels himself hindered by enemies. Ingrams knew that Raffan's own desire was to be one of the new boys he belittled, but as long as the material was new, and true, there was no loss to him in the arrangement. Of course, it was not an ideally disinterested form of

commentary – but few political articles other than straightforward news reports, can claim to be wholly free of bias.
Ingrams recognised that in Raffan the *Eye* had found a man
who would write about politicians with feline ruthlessness.
His 'New Boys' column punished all freshmen seekers after
power, some more venomously than others. Raffan rarely
visited the *Eye*, and until the *Guardian* diary story never had
his name linked with the disreputable denizens of Greek
Street. Although his old employer, Lady Olga Maitland,
nicknamed him 'Raffish', there was nothing happy-go-
lucky or carefree about Raffan.

He saw that the *Eye* would be useful to him, accepted
cheerfully the role in which he was cast, fulfilled his brief
brilliantly – then dumped the *Eye* when it threatened to
prove an embarrassment to him. His role was later filled by
Christopher Silvester, who also wanted to become a Tory
MP. But Silvester got into the *Eye* pigsty well over his
silver-grey spats. Raffan was indiscrete, but selectively so;
Silvester lacks this talent for discrimination.

Everyone was fair game to 'The Spiv', as Silvester is
known, even employers on the point of hiring him. In 1986
he scored a notable bullseye in this respect. He was asked
by a journalist-entrepreneur to join a proposed new
evening paper; but his proposed employer had had a
number of unfortunate business reverses in this field in the
past, which had been recorded in the *Eye*. Silvester suggested that the air should be cleared, and set about writing
an article for Fleet Street's trade magazine the *UK Press
Gazette* which, while noting these past reverses, would set
them in a proper context against the thrilling prospects of
the new paper. Somewhere along the line Silvester's in-
corrigible indiscretion took possession of him, and his out-
line of the past difficulties formed a major part of what was
intended as a laudatory article. The chief financial backer of
the paper saw the piece and decided to back out. Within
hours of hearing the news Silvester was merrily laughing
about the debacle. Raffan would never have made that
mistake. He was an effective sniper, while Silvester remains

the kind of man who is prone to shooting himself in the toe.

Christopher Booker and John Wells are perhaps the only men who have managed to continue contributing to the *Eye* while remaining equivocal about much of the magazine's content. Booker has often deplored much of the news and gossip material that appears in *Private Eye* – privately and in print – but he has never considered it necessary to leave; neither has Ingrams, who values Booker's contributions to the joke pages, frozen him out. If this means that Booker has to carry a burden of hypocrisy, then it must be said that it is lightly borne. Around the office he is a cheery, be-spectacled soul, who puts one in mind of those fey clerics who make an annual pilgrimage to the Walsingham shrine. His *Who's Who* entry is revealing. He makes the point that he was 'resident' scriptwriter on the 1960s satire show *That Was The Week That Was*, which neatly sets him apart from the legion of hacks who merely sent in jokes. He mentions all of his books, and tells how, between 1972 and 1977, he wrote extensively about property development, planning and housing in collaboration with Benny Gray, who went on to open pizza parlours. He mentions only his *third* wife, Valerie, whom he married in 1979. In 1962 he had married Emma Tennant, a member of the upper classes who, he told Marnham later, 'had taken us up'. At Cambridge Booker had said he wanted to marry a duke's daughter, edit his own paper and appear on television. Emma Tennant was not quite a duke's daughter, but she was an interesting aristocrat. Their wedding party was held at the home of Mark and Arabella Boxer in Kensington, and a guest des-cribed it thus in Marnham's history of the *Eye*:

> The highlight was a drag act by two window dressers from C & A. They wore chandelier earings, they were dressed as cinema usherettes and they sang a song with the refrain,
>
> > Would you like a lick of my lollipop?
> > Would you like a suck on my sweet?

Miss Tennant was then a left-winger, memorably described by former *Eye* contributor Maurice Hatton as 'The girl who put the Che in Cheyne Walk'. Booker had not then entered his thoughtful middle years, during which he was to describe his chief recreation as 'Jungian philosophy' and when Ingrams would nickname him 'The Deacon'.

While finding it a most congenial outlet for his whimsies, Booker is intolerant of *Eye* material which makes fun of his friends. In particular, he was aghast at gossip about his old Cambridge friend Arianna Stassinopoulos. Booker was one of the clever men Miss Stassinopoulos had consulted when she embarked on her determined crash course in understanding London's literary and publishing scene.

Ingrams, contemptuous of what he saw as Booker's weakness for wealthy people, made sure that the *Eye* was not short of material about 'the Greek pudding'. He told me in 1986 that 'Booker always falls for phonies, and I'm afraid he is also a bit of a backstabber. Mary never spoke to him after the article in the *Spectator* about the Dick West case.' Their relationship is strictly a professional one. Booker is a keen cricket fan, but he has never been invited to the *Eye*'s annual match. Ingrams is derogatory in a good-natured way about Booker's journalism outside the *Eye*, especially his 'God slot' pieces in the *Daily Telegraph*. When I recently became editor of *Sunday Today*, for which Booker writes a weekly comment column, Ingrams advised: 'Sack him. He's no good.'

This was suggested in joking terms, but Ingrams was at least half serious and repeated the advice for weeks. When he saw that the Booker column continued to appear, he said to me one day: 'Booker says you have no power on that paper – you can't hire or fire.' I said he was telling me this to goad me into proving Booker incorrect in the most dramatic fashion. He laughingly agreed, but continued to urge: 'Dump the Deacon.' Silvester made sure that Booker knew in detail about these discussions.

John Wells has similarly ambiguous relationship with the *Eye*. He came in to write 'Dear Bill' with Ingrams, but disapproves of much of the other material. Once he strode into Ingrams' office and declared: 'Well, Dempster has finally done it – he's killed a man.' The Greatest Living Englishman had written an offensive story about a family, and an elderly member of it had died shortly afterwards. There was no connection whatever between the 'Grovel' story and the man's death.

Along with Booker, he used the Marnham book to distance himself from the news and gossip sections of *Private Eye*. Ingrams thinks of Wells as a social climber and a snob, and their humorous collaboration has not been free of strife. When 'Dear Bill' proved a success, Wells proposed a stage version; but they could not agree on the format. Ingrams wanted a small production that would remain true to the original. Wells had grander plans, and eventually wrote his own comedy with a large cast, which did well at the Whitehall Theatre.

Ingrams boycotted the opening night, and urged the view that the play was 'piss-poor', a favoured term of dismissal he had picked up from Sir John Junor. He planted stories in various gossip columns about how much money Wells was making from what had begun as a joint idea. He believed Wells had coarsened the idea of Denis Thatcher in the play in order to make it more accessible to people who did not read *Private Eye*.

Ingrams was also scornful of the fact that the play's impresario was Paul Raymond, whom he regarded as unacceptably sleazy. He considered it a rich joke that Margaret Thatcher turned up with Denis to see the play, and was obliged afterwards to invite Raymond, who is also the proprietor of a striptease show, to a party at Number Ten.

Wells succeeded where others had failed in that he all but hijacked a *Private Eye* joke and made it his own. He performed the part of Denis on TV ('piss-poor' – Ingrams) and in a James Bond film ('piss-poor' – Ingrams). The idea of Denis Thatcher being a steady drinker had been, and remained, a major feature of the 'Dear Bill' letter. But outside the pages of *Private Eye*, Wells's portrayal of the boozy prime ministerial consort was rather one-dimensional.

Of all the *Eye*'s contributors John Wells knows best how to play Ingrams. He knows what is wanted and how to provide it, and he uses the *Eye* to the best advantage. He and Ingrams also produced 'Mrs Wilson's Diary', and after Mrs Thatcher there is every likelihood that they will collaborate again to render comic, pathetic and risible the next occupant of Number Ten. Like many comic teams, they do not socialise with one another, and they are not close friends.

Twenty-five years on it is remarkable that the Shrewsbury four – Ingrams, Booker, Rushton and Foot – still collaborate to produce *Private Eye*. But only the friendship of Ingrams and Foot has remained close. Together, they have the ease of friends who have gone separate ways in life, argued over many things, yet remain united by a deep bond of shared memories and beliefs.

Booker and Rushton both enjoyed periods when they were better known than Ingrams, especially during the days of *That Was The Week That Was*, in which they were stars – Willie as a performer, mimicking Harold Macmillan, and Booker as a writer. But both would resent the way Ingrams came to embody *Private Eye*.

In Booker's case, this found expression during the big public controversies in which *Private Eye*, and Ingrams, took on powerful outside enemies. Booker sided against them in the Goldsmith case, and once said that as far as he was concerned *Private Eye* could be seen as one of the most unpleasant things in journalism. There is no doubt that Booker was perfectly sincere in his misgivings about the way Ingrams conducted the Goldsmith case personally. But his grounds for biting the hand that fed him, certainly in the Goldsmith case, seem slim in retrospect, and open to the suspicion that he was jealous of Ingrams' highly-publicised position in the cockpit of controversy.

Rushton never publicly attacked *Private Eye*, or Ingrams. Even his outburst 'About time, too!' when Ingrams announced his retirement was taken as a joke. He continues to draw for the *Eye*, and to illustrate *Eye* books. He rarely comes into the office, but he is invited to parties, and to the Ingrams home for the annual cricket matches. Their friendship is not close, but it is usually civil.

In some ways it is odd that only Ingrams and Foot remain close thirty years after they met at Shrewsbury. The views of Booker and Ingrams have developed roughly in the same way: both have become increasingly enamoured of Malcolm Muggeridge, the *Daily Telegraph* and God.

Paul Foot left Shrewsbury as a socialist, and has not deviated from this path. He has written and delivered speeches on behalf of the far-left Socialist Workers' Party, he lives in a housing association property in north London, and he continues tirelessly to attack what he sees as the citadels of power and privilege.

He has worked full-time for *Private Eye* twice, leaving on both occasions because he found he could not exert enough control over his space and on what was published. He has often disapproved of gossip and joke material designed to bait progressive opinion – such as the story portraying battered wives' hostel pioneer Erin Pizzey as a 'lard mountain' who had given her ex-husband a severe financial mauling after a divorce. Yet he has never attacked Ingrams either publicly or privately. Neither will he disclose anything he knows of Ingrams' private life. When Ingrams stayed for two months with Paul and Rose Foot following his brief separation from Mary in the 1970s, it would never have occurred to Foot to gossip about their marital problems, even though the story would have been reported enthusiastically in the progressive organs to which he contributed, and which had been attacked by *Private Eye*. Foot considers such stories distasteful, wherever they appear.

Ingrams and Foot found they could not work together on anything approaching a full-time basis, but Foot buckled down cheerfully to the anonymous, poorly-rewarded role of 'pro rata contributor', and he has been a constant and reliable supplier of stories. But his position is not an entirely philanthropic one. He has found the *Eye* a receptive organ for Thatcher-bashing stories – so long as they are *stories* and not pure commentary.

Given Ingrams' informal policy of savaging those employers who give work to *Eye* contributors, Foot has often found himself having to tread a delicate line because of divided loyalties. In the 1980s he started an investigative column on the *Daily Mirror*, while that paper was owned by the giant paper firm Reed International. Then the *Mirror* was bought by socialist millionaire Robert Maxwell, whom Foot had previously attacked bitterly in the pages of the *Eye*. The *Eye* stepped up its attacks on Maxwell, inaugurating a cartoon strip, 'Captain Bob', ridiculing the new *Mirror* boss for his alleged megalomania and ineptitude.

Foot has never complained about the *Eye*'s torrent of anti-Maxwell jokes and lampoons, but his position inside the *Mirror* is a precarious one, especially since Maxwell has embarked on a course of litigation against the *Eye* which promises to rival the Goldsmith saga. Foot continues to bring round his copy on the Friday or Monday of publication week, often achieving the difficult task of writing new material for both the *Mirror* and the *Eye* on the same running story.

In the summer of 1986 he was consumed with the story of John Stalker, a senior policeman who was taken off an inquiry into killings of Roman Catholics by members of the Royal Ulster Constabulary. Stalker was suspended after being accused of consorting with criminals, but Foot believed passionately that the accusations were trumped up by the government to inhibit the Ulster inquiry. He wrote about the case in his *Mirror* column and in the front section of *Private Eye*. His *Eye* material was much more pointed – like other powerful newspapers, the *Mirror* has a small appetite for litigation. Foot used the *Eye* to keep the story rolling, a technique which has been used by other journalists who have contributed simultaneously to the *Eye* and a national newspaper.

He had done this on many occasions, notably during the

Helen Smith affair. Foot believed that this young nurse's 'accidental' death by falling from a parapet during a party in Saudi Arabia had been hushed up by the Foreign Office to protect local Britons.

Foot believed the government was capable of having troublesome individuals murdered, and that the secret intelligence services were often involved in subverting the course of political life. Back in the 1960s he had used the *Eye* to attack the Tory government of the day over the James Hanratty murder case, because he believed an innocent man had been hanged. Ingrams shared this belief that governments could act with astonishing ruthlessness, though he was less fervent on the subject than Foot. Ingrams told me he thought that the 1950s Labour leader Hugh Gaitskell had been murdered by the intelligence services when it looked as if he might live to succeed the ailing Tory Prime Minister of that time, Harold Macmillan. He also believed that Helen Smith's death was not accidental.

On the one hand he had Foot and others – notably the investigative journalist Jack Lundin, who had worked in Saudi Arabia – amassing details of the extraordinary events surrounding the party in Saudi Arabia; on the other hand Foreign Office officials were letting him know 'off the record' that there was nothing in it. At that time the small ads section of *Private Eye* was handled by Sarah Burns, whose husband Andrew was an astute, high-flying Foreign Office official working for Foreign Secretary Lord Carrington. The Burnses were embarrassed by the Helen Smith affair. But the official story that there was nothing in it was, if anything, counter-productive – as was the seemingly casual social visit of a senior FO official to the Ingrams' home in Berkshire, who told the same story.

Ingrams continued to believe Paul Foot long after public interest in the story had died. He trusted the instincts of his old schoolfriend. He balanced Foot's enthusiasm for stories which illustrated the ruthlesssness of power-seeking men against the soothing, contradictory Establishment noises to the effect that those who ran *Private Eye* and those who worked at the FO – or any government department – were the same kind of chaps at the end of the day. And he found for Foot.

They are a delightful pair at lunch. Foot disproves abundantly the idea that left-wing socialists do not have a sense of humour and are unable to laugh at themselves. He likes to mimic hypocritical Tories, sounding as he does so like an absurdly right-wing duke. But he is pleased, too, with Ingrams' impressions of Foot's self-seeking, left-wing brothers. The Gay Hussar table at which we often met on Fridays would rock with laughter as they vied with each other to perform conversational skits on stories of the day.

Foot is the only *Eye* contributor, or friend of Ingrams, who can gatecrash an Ingrams lunch to which he has not been invited and be sure of a warm welcome. Not that he is a natural gatecrasher – he is a polite and courteous man. He loves to gossip, and once got me to start a column called 'Philby' in the *Socialist Worker*. This was intended to print stories about the personal excesses of tycoons, but it was unpopular among some of Foot's more purist colleagues. Ingrams brought it to an end by printing a story which revealed that I was the author of the column – an item he knew would not find favour with my employer at the time, *Daily Express* proprietor Lord Matthews, for whom I was writing 'William Hickey'.

Ingrams was occasionally the unwitting source of stories about Foot in diary columns. While I was at the *Standard* in 1986 he mentioned to me that Foot had told him proudly that his son had joined the picket around Rupert Murdoch's printing plant at Wapping. I mentioned this to the editor of the *Standard*'s 'Londoner's Diary' column, who thought it worthy of mention. But Foot senior declined to confirm the story and the item was dropped. He did call Ingrams, who later telephoned me to report cheerfully: 'You've got me into trouble with Footie.'

Foot told Marnham for the official history that he liked *Private Eye*'s independence, and he said of Ingrams:

At *Private Eye*'s reserved table at the Coach & Horses: (*left to right*) Martin Tomkinson (hack), Richard Ingrams (Lord Gnome), Auberon Waugh (diarist) and Nigel Dempster ('Grovel').

In happier days: (*left to right*) Jeffrey Bernard ('Colonel Mad'), Martin Tomkinson and Richard Ingrams.

Former *Eye* diarist Auberon Waugh – a man who, according to Tony 'Toady' Shrimsley does not 'deserve to share the company of decent people' – 'dances' at a Playboy party hosted by Victor 'Disgusting' Lownes.

Nigel Dempster – once the 'Greatest Living Englishman' but now 'Humpty-Dumpster' or 'Pratt-Dumpster' – with author Peter McKay at the Epsom Derby.

The *Eye*'s principal shareholder, suave comedian Peter Cook, introduced to Princess Michael of Kent, who doesn't know which way to turn.

Richard West, whose book *Victory in Vietnam* – co-published by *Private Eye* – initiated one of the most acrimonious legal battles in the magazine's history.

Ingrams' dislike of the legal profession stops short at ex-Master of the Rolls Lord Denning, who wholeheartedly supported the *Eye* in the legal battles with Goldsmith.

Eye designer Tony Rushton with his wife and Mary Ingrams, who calls her husband 'Ditch' and, some say, rules *Private Eye* from their Berkshire home.

Christopher 'The Deacon' Booker with his wife and Nigel Dempster at the *Eye*'s twenty-first anniversary party.

Sir Peter Jay, a long-time supporter of the *Eye*, with the magazine's resident socialist and Ingrams' closest friend, Paul Foot.

Vintage *Eye* characters: 'Fragrant Doyenne' Lady Olga Maitland and the persistent mouth organist Larry Adler.

Cartoonist Michael Heath ('Great Bores' and 'The Gays') comforts tired colleague Frank Dickens.

Christopher Logue ('True Stories' and 'Pseud's Corner') tries one out on *Eye* shareholder Bernard Braden.

Richard Ingrams dances with Candida Lycett Green at the *Eye*'s twenty-first anniversary celebrations. 'It is difficult to explain how wonderful he is,' she sighed, 'but he exudes goodness and a faint holiness.'

I think he is a brilliant editor, although I can't bear his prejudices, which get worse as he gets older . . . The paper is still admirable. It could never have been left-wing. But again and again it comes out on top because he will publish things that other people won't.

Certainly that was true for Paul Foot. Ingrams' patience on a long-running story was not inexhaustible, but if Foot could come up with any new angle he would keep battering away at a scandal. They had learned to live happily with one another, and preserve their close friendship.

This extended to Paul Foot's uncle, Michael Foot. He had had his share of abuse in *Private Eye*, but it was noticeably more gentle and lacking in real venom than the attacks on his predecessors as head of the Labour party. Michael Foot became 'Worzel', named after Keith Waterhouse's brilliant TV creation, the scarecrow Worzel Gummidge. Ingrams loved to gossip about Michael Foot privately, but Worzel never became a 'Grovel' target.

Chapter Four

In the Dock

'It is extraordinary how keen people are that someone else should attack *Private Eye*,' observed a *Sunday Times* columnist, reporting on the magazine's twentieth anniversary party in 1981. Perhaps it is not so extraordinary: there is no shortage of people who would like to see *Private Eye* laid low, but the number of those who are prepared to have a go themselves – and thereby risk becoming the subject of one of the *Eye*'s notoriously persistent campaigns of vilification – is rather smaller.

One of the few politicians from whom *Private Eye* has drawn writs for libel – though the issue was not in itself political – was Winston Churchill's son Randolph. In 1963 they composed a lampoon about 'The Greatest Dying Englishman', suggesting that Randolph's life's work, a biography of his father, was being ghost-written by hacks who would steer clear of controversial events in the great man's life – such as Gallipoli, Dieppe and the sending of police to a miners' strike at Tonypandy.

The affair drew massive publicity, which the *Eye* exploited by mounting a display of the legal paraphernalia of writs, letters and so forth – which was then unfamiliar to them – in the window. But the magazine was sufficiently worried by the writs for business manager Nicholas Luard to journey to Suffolk to see Randolph, taking Willie Rushton with him in the hope that Willie would amuse the disgruntled biographer. After five hours, it was agreed that the *Eye* would withdraw its comments in a full page of the *Evening Standard*. This took the form of a letter from Randolph to the *Eye*, which began: 'Sir, I call your attention to the lies and libels about my father and myself contained in your issue of February 8 . . .' At the end of his catalogue of grievances was the statement:

> We, the undersigned, wish to withdraw the false allegations implied against Sir Winston and Randolph Churchill, and the latter's assistants in the issue of *Private Eye* of February 8th.

The *Eye* had got off lightly, and they emerged from the experience feeling triumphant. Nicholas Luard told Marnham:

> Until then we had been hanging on the coat tails of the satire boom. After that we were on our own . . . we increased the print order.

There followed the Profumo Affair, in which the *Eye* played a part by providing its readers with a regular diet of nudges and winks about naughtiness in high places. But perhaps it was the row with Randolph Churchill that set them up for the years of controversy that were to follow. They learned that this kind of hit-and-run, revelatory journalism was fun, and that it was possible for a vigorous if small magazine to cut through the cosy conspiracies of Fleet Street and Westminster. Their enemies from then on became the power-seekers who concealed their ulterior motives and self-serving actions behind a cloak of elevated sentiments.

As the years passed, Ingrams came to understand the crucial importance when attacking a target of homing in on their lawyers and supporters at the same time. He understood that these peripheral figures would be less likely to urge retaliatory action against *Private Eye* if they knew that they too would have to line up in the shooting gallery when the battle was joined.

Thus Lord Goodman, the eminent solicitor who acted for Harold Wilson and Lady Falkender, was for years a frequent target of *Eye* gossip and jokes. In the 1980s the *Eye* found another legal target, Peter Carter-Ruck, by then London's leading libel solicitor, whose name adorned many of the documents that arrived at their Carlisle Street offices. Carter-Ruck became 'Carter-Fuck', the 'avaricious solicitor'. Friends of the solicitor told Ingrams that there were many things that could be said in Carter-Ruck's favour, and that he had refrained from suing the *Eye* personally because he had a sneaking regard for the magazine. In the early years of his career, before the introduction of Legal Aid, he had acted as a poor man's lawyer, and had accepted other unpaid duties on behalf of the legal profession. This cut no ice with Ingrams, whose long experience of litigation left him more or less chronically anti-lawyer. He was much tickled by a remark I remembered – possibly from Mark Twain: 'The mere title of lawyer is enough to deprive a man of public confidence.'

His biggest-ever case combined in equal measure politics, high society and lawyers. Sir James Goldsmith was the principal protagonist, but supporting roles in the drama were assigned to Harold Wilson and Goldsmith's lawyer, Eric Levine.

In November 1975 Ingrams was intrigued to read a newspaper story about a requiem mass at the Jesuit Church in Farm Street, Mayfair, for Dominic Elwes, an artist and socialite who had killed himself two months previously. An odd-sounding address had been given at the service by gambling club and zoo owner John Aspinall, supposedly a friend of Elwes. Aspinall reportedly said that Elwes's genetic inheritance had left him ill-equipped for life. A cousin of Elwes punched Aspinall in the face outside the church after the mass.

Elwes had, in fact, fallen out with Aspinall in the months before his death by assisting a *Sunday Times* journalist, James Fox, to prepare a sensational article about the Lucan case. In November 1974 Lucan, a member of Aspinall's

Clermont Club circle of gambling friends, had broken into his wife's house and killed the nanny, supposedly mistaking her for his wife. He had then disappeared off the face of the earth. Introduced to Fox by Elwes, Aspinall made some rather quotable remarks about the Lucan affair, and in particular the character of the missing earl. He said Lucan – 'like myself' – was 'born out of his time . . . a model that would have been better exposed in the early nineteenth century. . . His qualities, as they appeared to me, were the old-fashioned qualities, like loyalty, honesty and reliability.'

He went on to pour contempt on Lady Lucan, and said that he had told the police who had interviewed him: 'If she'd been my wife I'd have bashed her to death five years before, and so would you.' He also told Fox that he would have helped Lucan on the murder night if he had been asked to do so: 'If a close friend of yours came in covered with blood, having done some frightful deed, the last thing that would have occurred to you is to turn him in.'

The subsequent article caused a sensation, not least at the Clermont Club. Fox took the side of Lady Lucan and portrayed Aspinall and his friends as 'weird and thoroughly unpleasant people'. Elwes, to whom Fox paid £200 for his help, was mortified – especially since one of his own paintings was used to illustrate the colour magazine piece. This showed Lucan sitting with his cronies at the Clermont – including Elwes, Aspinall and James Goldsmith. In the aftermath, Elwes was banned from both the Clermont and Annabel's (a fashionable nightclub in the basement of the Clermont), both central to his life, and he killed himself. He left behind a note saying: 'I curse Mark [Birley, owner of Annabel's] and Jimmy from beyond the grave. I hope they are happy now.'

Briefed by Ingrams and Nigel Dempster on the story, Patrick Marnham headlined his *Eye* article about the affair: 'All's Well That Ends Elwes.' It began: 'From the beginning police have met obstruction and silence from the circle of gamblers and boneheads with whom Lord Lucan and

Dominic Elwes associated.' He went on to suggest that a lunch held by the Clermont set on the day after the murder had been chaired by Goldsmith to discuss what had happened and, if possible, help Lord Lucan. Since Elwes was the only one who had remained a friend of Veronica Lucan, he was sent to St George's Hospital, were she was recovering from the ordeal, to talk to her.

Marnham also drew attention to the fact Greville Howard, an Old Etonian member of the Clermont set, a business associate of Goldsmith and an intimate of Lord Lucan, had earlier told police that he had heard Lucan speak of his intention to murder Lady Lucan. But at the time of the inquest he had entered the Nuffield Clinic for treatment to his back, and did not give this vital evidence to the inquest on the dead nanny. Howard had worked for Goldsmith at Slater Walker, the city investment bankers taken over by the financier following a crisis and the sudden resignation of its controversial founder, James Slater. He had earlier been Goldsmith's personal assistant.

In essence, the *Private Eye* story was a fascinating mélange of fact and surmise. Did Goldsmith 'obstruct' police inquiries into the Lucan case? Was he a fit person for the Bank of England to appoint as the saviour of Slater Walker? Marnham's story concluded cheerily:

> Given the vote of confidence which the city has recently given Jimmy, he probably is quite happy, and there seems to be no reason to question the Bank of England's stated confidence in him as a man of integrity, well fitted to guide the helm of a great public enterprise.

Ingrams says of the story in his fascinating book *Goldenballs*: 'In spite of the rather frantic conditions in which it was put together, I counted the article a success . . .'

Private Eye is different from most Fleet Street papers in one crucial respect. Once it has got hold of what Ingrams considers a good story, it goes on about it issue after issue. In Fleet Street there is a tendency to have one crack at a story, then drop it – allegedly for fear of boring the readers. In fact, an unresolved story is more likely to be dropped because of the low boredom threshold of the journalists involved, or because of mounting panic in the paper's legal department. Ingrams did not find the story boring; nor was he panicked by the prospect of legal proceedings.

For the next issue, Ingrams drafted in the *Eye*'s city expert, Michael (Slicker) Gillard. He not only cast doubt on Goldsmith's independence of James Slater, but also added a detail about Goldsmith's solicitor, Eric Levine. Gillard disclosed that Levine was a director of two Goldsmith companies, as well as having been associated at one time – innocently – with T. Dan Smith, a businessman then in prison for bribing councillors in the north-east.

Ingrams recalls:

> It . . . came as something of a surprise when on 12 January, three days after the issue containing the Levine article was published, Goldsmith issued sixty-three writs, against *Private Eye* and over thirty of our distributors, and applied to the High Court to bring proceedings for criminal libel in respect of the Elwes article.

In his criminal libel affidavit, Goldsmith disclosed a fact that stunned Ingrams: he had *not* been present at the Clermont Club lunch following Lucan's disappearance. How, therefore, could he have been connected with the subsequent visit of Elwes to Lady Lucan's hospital room – which had given Marnham grounds for his conjecture that a conspiracy was involved?

There was also a problem over Marnham's use of the word 'obstruction'. The *Eye* was advised that it would have been far safer from a legal point of view if Marnham had written 'non-co-operation': obstructing the police is an offence; refusing to co-operate with them is not. The Marnham article had been toned down – by Ingrams and the *Eye*'s duty lawyer – on the day before publication, but both had overlooked 'obstruction'.

Two years and thirteen court hearings later the *Eye*–Goldsmith litigation was settled. The *Eye* agreed to contribute £30,000 over ten years to Goldsmith's costs and, as in the case of Randolph Churchill, a full-page apology was placed in the *Evening Standard*. But Ingrams felt the *Eye* had won.

Certainly the case benefited *Eye* sales, which had dropped by 12,000 at the commencement of the litigation. It stiffened the sinews of the magazine, and sharpened the lure of dangerous content – which for many readers was its most potent attraction.

Attending the various cases I was struck by the contrast between Ingrams and Goldsmith. Goldsmith was dressed expensively in the uniform of the international businessman – beautifully-cut dark suit, white shirt and silk tie. He always looked well scrubbed (if flushed), and he smoked Havana cigars. Although they were much the same age – Ingrams was born in 1937, Goldsmith in 1933 – they looked to be from different generations. Ingrams, with his acne scars and his old clothes, seemed like a student demonstrator summoned to court following a scuffle with a local bigwig. But in other ways he seemed much older and wiser than Goldsmith. He gave evidence in a calm, dignified way, never seeking, it seemed to me, to prevaricate when he did not know the answer to a question; Goldsmith, by contrast, blustered, lost his temper, and was advised by one judge to be 'less theatrical'. Ingrams behaved as if he had all the time in the world, and was engaged in a struggle that would last out his lifetime; Goldsmith appeared eager for the matter to be resolved, as if it were a trivial matter that was trespassing unnecessarily on his valuable executive time. No doubt this was true. But the case was important to Ingrams, too. The future of the magazine was in the balance. If he and Patrick Marnham went to prison – which was a possibility if the criminal libel case succeeded – the *Eye* might have closed, because Ingrams had made no provision for such an eventuality.

Several of the usually hidden animosities of English

society also came to the surface during the case. Ingrams was supported by country society, while Goldsmith was the jet set's candidate. There was also the Jewish question. Ingrams noted that two of the legal luminaries who acted against the *Eye* – Goldsmith's QC Lewis Hawser and Judge Wien – were from Cardiff Jewish backgrounds. Goldsmith was also seen as Jewish, as was his solicitor Eric Levine, whom Ingrams described as 'small, insignificant looking and smartly dressed'. Ingrams also noted that Hawser had anglicised his name from Hauser.

The picture emerged: old English county society versus *parvenu*, middle European Jews. *Private Eye* also had the support of the *Daily Telegraph* and its editor William Deedes, himself from an ancient Kentish landowning family. One of the team of barristers supporting the *Eye* was Desmond Browne, a member of the vast Irish Guinness family. There was an interesting scene in one court hearing. Lewis Hawser admitted that Goldsmith had gone through *Private Eye*'s dustbins in search of evidence, and Browne asked the judge (in vain) to require Sir James to return from a Corsican holiday to explain further this fascinating episode. The two men were usually accompanied by their wives, Lady Annabel Goldsmith and Mary Ingrams. Here again there was a fascinating picture of contrasting women. Lady Annabel was often attired in sexily-split dresses, beloved of Fleet Street press photographers, and high-heeled shoes. Mary said she looked 'tarty', and dressed herself in sensible, country gentlewoman clothes. She glared repeatedly at her opposite number.

Both the Goldsmiths and the Ingramses were middle-class. Jimmy Goldsmith had gone to Eton, a cut above Shrewsbury in the public schools hierarchy, but he had not gone to university. He had scored his first financial success by placing an accumulator bet while still a schoolboy at Eton. Now he was a highly organised, energetic man who had become a millionaire through shrewd business dealings. He jetted between New York, Paris and London, kept a mistress, and sought, through the acquisition of newspapers, to become a public force in the country.

He had formed a fascinating friendship with Harold Wilson and his all-powerful private secretary Marcia Williams. It was widely reported that he had been listed for a peerage in Williams' notorious 'Lavender List', but that this had been downgraded to a knighthood. But why should this evidently Tory millionaire have been put forward by a Labour premier for an honour in the first place? Officially it was for his services to 'export and ecology'. But *Evening Standard* Paris correspondent Sam White, an old friend of Goldsmith, later told Ingrams he thought the knighthood was Wilson's and Williams' way of thanking Jimmy for taking on *Private Eye*, which had for years made them and their administration a laughing stock. His contribution to ecology was his attempt to clean up the environment, as they saw it, by removing *Private Eye*.

The outcome of the case was satisfactory to *Private Eye* in one particular way that was not appreciated fully at the time: no constraints were put upon articles about Goldsmith in the future. Moreover, as in all litigation, the Goldsmith–*Private Eye* affair yielded a mountain of information under the 'discovery' rules about both organisations. Ingrams was determined to use it. While Goldsmith had the satisfaction of confirming his suspicion that several Fleet Street journalists were active supporters of *Private Eye*, Ingrams, and more importantly Michael (Slicker) Gillard, had an incomparably richer treasure trove of documentation about the infrastructure of Goldsmith's companies.

Goldsmith was portrayed in the press as the winner in the case, and indeed that was technically accurate. But quite apart from the fact that his business dealings were laid open to Slicker's hungry gaze, Goldsmith lost a great deal in subtle ways that were not amenable to press explanation at the time. He had wanted to become a public figure in Britain, and a publisher of newspapers and magazines. *Private Eye*'s exposure of him in court was not helpful in this respect. A few enemies of the *Eye* cheered him on; but their support did not compare with those who poured £40,000 into the *Eye*'s 'Goldenballs' fund.

Those who had been victims of Ingrams intransigence might well have sympathized with Goldsmith at the end of the day. Here was a big, tough, wealthy man with batteries of lawyers and bags of energy and determination, yet the best he could get out of it all was an *Evening Standard* apology and a contribution to his costs. Some of the women at *Private Eye* confessed that they found Jimmy sexy, and sympathetic. Ingrams was greatly amused by this (his wife Mary less so). There were indications from time to time that Goldsmith wanted to be friendly, to meet Ingrams. But Ingrams has a tough nature and he would never have agreed to it.

In the end Ingrams was able to exercise the kind of power Goldsmith probably never dreamed *Private Eye* possessed. He could dedicate his magazine to hounding Goldsmith issue after issue with his traditional double-pronged weapon of damaging revelations and humiliating jokes. Goldsmith has probably never met such a deadly enemy.

It is a difficult art to hate a man yet at the same time make effective jokes about him: you either hate him too much and the jokes have a bitter edge; or you don't hate him enough and the jokes are only so-so. Ingrams hated Goldsmith, Wilson *et al*, and all he thought they stood for, with a quiet passion, but he was capable of coming back from court and writing spoofs about them that would keep readers roaring with laughter.

Goldsmith had some success in tempering the criticism of himself in orthodox newspapers by appealing to their proprietors. That could hardly work in the case of *Private Eye*. He tried persuading journalists to take up the cudgels against the magazine, but was unsuccessful. His failure to destroy *Private Eye* was especially galling because it had the reverse effect – as the endless roll-call of names of contributors to the 'Goldenballs' fund published in the magazine each fortnight bore witness.

Goldsmith left Britain for America, and France, where he owned *L'Express* magazine and enjoyed dual French-British citizenship. For years he was an outcast from the ranks of potential press barons. Yet from time to time Slicker has reminded readers of his new moves. There has been no escape with Ingrams at the helm. But will *Private Eye* go soft on Goldsmith and his kind when Hislop takes over, as part of the magazine's avowed intention to reduce the libel bill? Certainly it is difficult to imagine Hislop engaging in mortal combat with so mighty an enemy and emerging not only unbowed, but healthier and more vigorous than before.

Goldsmith called the *Eye*'s relationship with Fleet Street, or a coterie of journalists there, 'symbiotic' – meaning that they feed off each other. This is true in a limited sense. Many journalists find the *Eye* bold and exciting, especially in an age when Fleet Street has become something of a sausage factory – owned by conglomerates, run by marketing men and producing a diet of safe and often uniform material, all too frequently about minor television personalities.

The *Eye* has no proprietor as such. It scorns soft news. Its definition of news is material that somebody doesn't want to see in print. Moreover, the *Eye* regards Fleet Street itself as news, and applies the same definition to stories from what it calls the 'Street of Shame'. Early on in its history, the *Eye* found that journalists who were ridiculed in its pages were quick to sue, usually with the financial assistance and backing of their papers.

Ingrams has never understood why journalists sue. He has often been attacked in newspapers, and when he considers that a response is necessary, or might be amusing, he torments his attackers in the *Eye*. Would he ever sue under any circumstances, I have often asked him. He replies that he cannot envisage a situation in which he would take that course.

He believes that if a story about you is false then there is no point in denying it or suing. Your friends and associates – those who matter to you – will know it is untrue, and therefore no harm has been done. When he fell out with

Nigel Dempster in 1986 he leaked fictitious and derogatory items about himself to Dempster's diary. One was to the effect that the *Eye* attacked Prince Charles because Ingrams was angry not to have been invited to his wedding. The items were sent to Dempster by Paul Halloran, who on one occasion gave the £50 cheque he received from the *Daily Mail* to Ingrams' daughter Jubby.

Ingrams says he cannot understand why hacks have proved so quick to take offence and so eager to sue. I have suggested that this might be because journalists, unlike most of their readers, believe what is printed in the papers.

Paul Johnson was one of the first of the *Eye*'s Fleet Street litigants. He sued 'Ingram [sic] and another' in 1968 when the *Eye* suggested that, while editor of the *New Statesman*, Johnson had adopted 'a fawning attitude' towards Harold Wilson, Labour premier at the time. In view of Johnson's later conversion from the left wing of the Labour Party to the right wing of the Conservatives, and his stout support for Margaret Thatcher, the 1968 case makes amusing reading today.

His counsel reminded the court that the *New Statesman* had a long and honourable history as a strong supporter of progressive principles and causes. Over a period of two years the *Eye* had sustained . . .

> . . . a scurrilous and malicious campaign in the form of gravely defamatory attacks on the plaintiffs, 14 of which are cited on the writ.

Looking back through these 'gravely defamatory' attacks now it is difficult to see what the fuss was about. Of course, lawyers, like salesman, do have to make inflated claims for their merchandise before a court. But it is hard not to conclude that Johnson was being a pompous fool. Nevertheless, he won the case.

As a journalist, humour has never been his forte. For years his speciality has been slashing polemical attacks on those who offend whatever code of ethics and customs he happens to be espousing at the time. These attacks were safe from the laws of libel since they could usually be protected under the rules of fair comment. The *Eye*'s campaign, such as it was, sought to suggest that the man behind the pen was a mean-spirited creature who fawned on those in power. Some who read his journalism twenty years on might consider this a prescient observation, in view of his articles about Rupert Murdoch and Margaret Thatcher. His friend Alan Watkins once wrote a friendly profile which said that Johnson 'felt the need to have both a party and a leader', and that 'he put his trust in princes'.

As with Goldsmith, *Private Eye* did not have to give an undertaking not to mention him again. But that distinction has been accorded to a number of journalists, notably Harold Evans, former editor of *The Sunday Times* and, briefly, *The Times*.

Evans hated being teased by *Private Eye*. But ironically he was an advocate of 'attack' journalism, and deplored the way in which powerful men and institutions would seek to 'gag' the press (usually himself) by issuing writs. At the same time he was able to use the resources of *The Sunday Times* to gag *Private Eye*. His case was that the *Eye* was telling lies about him, and that there could be no protection for liars. But he was sophisticated enough to know that libel law is not simply a question of lies and truth. Like all newspaper editors, he was personally indemnified by his newspaper group from the consequences of libels his paper published – part of his defence on one occasion was that he had not read a major article that had been published while he was in the chair.

In 1971 Evans got the diarist on the paper to print the names of those who attended *Private Eye*'s fortnightly lunches, presumably with the intention of scaring them off. Under a keyhole logo the *Sunday Times* 'Ear' diary reported:

The curious lunch where the magazine *Private Eye* gets much of its information takes place each Wednesday in the Coach and Horses pub in Greek Street. Here the invited finks sit around a long table and the reputations of such as Wilson and the Grocer and Ballsoff are examined over the wine, dusted up over the soup, bounced around over the main course and pulped over the coffee.

Presiding over the character assassinations and incestuous office prattle is the *Eye*'s editor, Richard (Give him another drink and he'll tell you all about Rhodesia) Ingrams. He is teetotal and is usually abetted by Paul Foot who, when the wine flows and the tongues loosen, takes out notebooks and jots down every word.

Ingrams says that three quarters of their contacts are in *The Sunday Times* but among those dining [sic] last Wednesday were Richard West, Michael Astor, Nemone Lethbridge, Neal Ascherson, Alan Watkins, Ann Chisholm, Andrew Osman [sic] and Patrick Garland.

Hardly household names but it is believed their presence is not unadjacent to what will be appearing in the next *Eye*. A pale, trembling Ingrams was last seen asking a reporter not to name any names but guest lists will be appearing in the Ear from time to time.

By a happy coincidence, Harold Evans' girlfriend (and eventually his wife) Tina Brown had first made her mark through associating with Auberon Waugh and the *Eye*. Bron had once brought her to the lunch, which she then wrote up in her university magazine. Later, when Evans' feud with *Private Eye* was well under way, Miss Brown, then editor of the *Tatler*, wrote about 'Lord Gnome's School for Scandal'. This rather breathless piece, in the fine tradition of Jean (Glenda Slag) Rook, began:

> Richard Ingrams is the headmaster of the School for Scandal but it's fruitless to have a pash on him. Even if you share your bun with him at break there's no guarantee it will penetrate his ironic reserve.

Miss Brown admitted that she had 'often mounted the creaking stairs of the Coach and Horses pub in Greek Street for the *Private Eye* lunch on Wednesdays'. She also said she had taken Ingrams to lunch at the Gay Hussar, and had asked one of his colleagues afterwards if he had enjoyed the experience. She was told: 'Quite . . . He used to regard you as rather a duchess figure. Now he thinks you're one of us.'

Miss Brown concluded primly:

Ingrams made me so pleased at passing the entrance exam I forgot to ask about the fees.

Neither Miss Brown nor Mr Evans were able to maintain a sense of humour about *Private Eye*. Both were fiercely ambitious, and they saw the *Eye* as an irritating obstacle. Miss Brown, like Mr Evans, was keen to dish out criticism, but childishly sensitive when her own character and habits were discussed in other than glowing terms. She specialised in glib, bitchy articles which depended for their success on making her victims – people she did not wish to suck up to – appear ridiculous. But when a critical paragraph once appeared in the *Evening Standard*'s 'Londoner's Diary' about a *Tatler* party she had organised, she rang Nigel Dempster in tears asking him to put matters right.

After many writs, Ingrams decided to go along with Evans' wishes – he agreed not to mention him, or Tina, in *Private Eye* again. Evans eventually fell out with his proprietor, Rupert Murdoch, and accepted a six-figure sum to leave the editor's chair at *The Times*. In 1983 he brought out a book, *Good Times, Bad Times*, excoriating the Murdoch style of proprietorship, and left to work in America.

Murdoch and Evans make an interesting contrast. *Private Eye* had ripped into Murdoch ever since he set foot in Britain in the 1960s, attributing the debasement of the Fleet Street press almost exclusively to his influence. To the *Eye* he was 'The Dirty Digger', coarse purveyor of bums and tits, and no effort was spared to make him appear a depraved and corrupt man. Yet Murdoch never sued *Private Eye*. He never wrote a letter of complaint. He never asked his newspapers to attack *Private eye*. When one of his newspapers mentioned the *Eye* favourably on rare occasions, he never castigated those responsible. Evans, on the other hand, sued

Private Eye many times. He was able to use the newspaper he edited to attack it, notably during the Thorpe case. He was anxious to weed out *Eye* informants at his newspapers. Eventually, his company's lawyers were able to obtain the undertaking from *Private Eye* that it would not mention him again.

Many regard Harold Evans as an admirable journalist. *The Sunday Times* has so far not recovered the flair that he brought to it as editor. He inspired some brilliant investigative journalism, and was rightly judged to be a great newspaper technician. Why was he so sensitive to *Private Eye*? One old friend and colleague said it was because 'Harry can't bear being laughed at'.

Ingrams said he was relieved in the end to enter into an undertaking not to mention Harry and Tina again because they had become boring. He loves paradox, and likes to argue that the undertaking was damaging to Evans and Brown in the end because at least people had talked about them when they featured in the *Eye*. Since they had gone to find fortune and fame in America everyone had forgotten them. There are elements of truth, but also of wishful thinking in this analysis.

Of all the weapons *Private Eye* employs to fight litigants, the most primitive is the 'Curse of Gnome', an arrangement whereby *Private Eye* exerts supposedly occult pressure on those who sue the magazine. Any subsequent misfortune – a broken elbow will do – is reported under a crude, 'Curse of Gnome' skull logo. The curse was once the subject of a bitter correspondence in *The Times* instituted by Patrick Hutber.

Hutber was a distinguished financial writer on the *Sunday Telegraph* and a friend of Sir James Goldsmith. At one time he sought to bring the *Eye*–Goldsmith wrangle to a close, believing – correctly some may think – that it was damaging the public standing of his friend. In June 1976, he wrote a letter to *The Times* which was given the heading 'Libelling the Dead':

Sir, anyone who is wondering whether or not to support *Private Eye*'s appeal for funds for legal expenses might consider an item in the current issue. It runs as follows: 'We regret to record that the dreaded Curse of Gnome has struck again. The action of *Killeen v Private Eye* (pending) has been terminated by the demise of Mr John Killeen, ARIBA.

'Mr Killeen was the architect who developed MACE, the building systems which provided special leaking schools all over London.' The item is tastefully illustrated with a skull and a quotation from Leviticus: 'You shall sow your seed in vain, for your enemies shall eat it.'

John Killeen, who died a few days before his 48th birthday last month, was a kind and gentle man, as I know from 43 happy and uninterrupted years of friendship with him. He was a fine architect, as a look at the London College of Printing will confirm. Within days of his death, and secure in the protection of the grave, *Private Eye* chooses to revive a grotesque libel for which it would have been punished in the courts.

Journalism is not enhanced by, nor does this country need, a magazine that has no higher idea of satire than to spit in the face of the dead.

The letter has a fine, indignant passion. But *Private Eye*'s reference to John Killeen, while tasteless, was not a 'grotesque libel'. It was true that a jury might have thought the *Eye* mistaken in its view of Killeen's work, but it is just as likely that they would have considered it fair comment. Patrick Hutber's letter relied heavily on the fact of his long friendship with a man he liked and approved of, and who was now dead. But Hutber knew better than most – through his friendship with Goldsmith – that *Private Eye* did not restrict itself to attacking the dead. It was their attack on Goldsmith on behalf of the dead Dominic Elwes that began their most epic libel action.

Hutber eventually went to work for Goldsmith's ill-fated *Now!* magazine. Auberon Waugh had been maintaining an appalling campaign against Anthony Shrimsley, editor of the magazine, and his brother Bernard, editor of the *News of the World*. Tony was 'Toady' and Bernard was 'Slimy'. I knew and liked Bernard (I had not met Tony), and it was very hard to justify some of Waugh's copy. But '*Talbot*' was featuring strongly in other pages of the *Eye*, too. Soon it was announced that the 'Curse of Gnome' had been placed on all the magazine's staff. Then Hutber was seriously injured in a road accident. Waugh wrote an unsympathetic piece in his diary. Soon afterwards, Hutber died.

Tony Shrimsley responded with a thundering leader in *Now!*, denouncing this 'piece of undiluted evil'. He wrote:

> My charge against Mr Waugh and Mr Ingrams is that they are not muckrakers but muckmakers. The lies, half truths and sheer inventions of *Private Eye* are now so all-pervading that it is impossible for any non-informed reader to disentangle whatever fact may be buried beneath them.

He went on to say that Waugh and Ingrams were 'wicked men . . . liars motivated by malice who do not deserve either to be employed as journalists or to share the company of decent people'.

It was perhaps the most passionately-written piece ever carried by the rather bland *Now!* But it was hard to regard the leader as an expression solely of pure and righteous indignation on Hutber's behalf since both Goldsmith and Shrimsley were such bitter enemies of *Private Eye*. Just as Hutber had done in the case of John Killeen, Tony Shrimsley was relying on Hutber's tragic death to rally opinion against *Private Eye*. There were plenty of other grounds on which to attack the *Eye* and the individuals who ran it, but Hutber and Shrimsley, it seems to me, both took the easy way out.

Private Eye's enemies have often proved rather gutless, either sheltering behind lawyers provided and paid for by their companies or in seeking to whip up public indignation through third parties. Anthony Howard, a former editor of the *New Statesman*, took this latter course during the Goldsmith struggles. He, too, wrote to *The Times*, saying *Private Eye* might have expected more support from him were it not for their treatment of his unfortunate colleague David Leitch.

David Leitch took *Private Eye* to court over Richard West's book *Victory in Vietnam*, which was co-published by André Deutsch and *Private Eye*. The book opened with a description of the death in Vietnam – in sordid circumstances – of an English journalist called Peter Duval-Smith. By the time West's book came out, David Leitch had married Jill Neville, Duval-Smith's widow. Duval-Smith and Jill Neville had an infant daughter and Leitch applied to the Family Division of the High Court for an injunction preventing distribution of the book – on the grounds that it was improper for the girl to grow up to read this account of her father's death. Initially, the court found in Leitch's favour; but the ruling was overturned on appeal, and Leitch was left with a bill for the costs.

Private Eye pursued Leitch with garnishee orders, seeking to sequester his *New Statesman* salary – and it was this move which provoked Howard's letter to *The Times*. Christopher Booker, a friend of Leitch, broke ranks (not for the first time) and wrote an article in the *Spectator* attacking *Private Eye*. Mary Ingrams never spoke to him again.

One might begin by asking why Howard, if he was really so indignant, did not have these costs paid for by the *New Statesman*. But there was another reason for regarding his letter to *The Times* as humbug: Howard would not have supported *Private Eye* in any circumstances, and had certainly never done so in the past, for he too had been a frequent subject of teasing in the *Eye*, where he had been nicknamed 'Nepalese' because of his faintly Oriental features.

Auberon Waugh wrote to *The Times* in reply to Howard's letter:

> Three quarters of cases brought against *Private Eye* are brought by fellow journalists. Any suggestion that special facilities be made available to journalists in the event of their losing would be disastrous for the *Eye*. If Mr Howard had been franker in his

approach, he might have suggested that this man be treated with exceptional mercy for the reason that unlike the usual run of journalistic hacks, dwarfs and illiterates who bring actions against the *Eye* he [Leitch] is a good journalist. On that point – and only on that point – I would agree that he has a case.

Instead of which, he delivers his kick in the ribs at a time when *Private Eye* faces the possibility of closure and its Editor the possibility of prison . . .

The Times played host to another attack on the *Eye*, this time from Cambridge lecturer Dr John Casey. His action against *Private Eye* was settled in his favour in 1986. Soon afterward's *The Times* printed an article about gossip written by Dr Casey, in which he made derogatory references to the *Eye*; the article ended with a short statement mentioning the litigation so that readers could judge for themselves how much, if at all, his experience with *Private Eye* had contributed to his thoughts on the subject.

Dr Casey, *Private Eye* claimed in its original article, had been found in bed with one of his male students, James Tregear. Mr Patrick Milmo QC said it was not sufficient to say the item was untrue; it was 'a mixture of total untruth, spurious gossip and scandal mongering' – 'one of the most scurrilous items' ever to have appeared in *Private Eye*. He was not going to refute the story line by line.

I will merely state that Dr Casey is a man of complete moral probity whose friendship with Mr Tregear is wholly normal and irreproachable.

Neither Mr Tregear nor Dr Casey has engaged in homosexual activities. No allegations could be more destructive of Dr Casey's professional and personal reputation than that he was sexually corrupting his students, and no accusation about Mr Tregear more unpleasant than that he was a promiscuous pervert.

Private Eye had published in the wake of the story several letters defending Dr Casey and Tregear. At first they were disposed to fight the action, raising a defence of justification. But this was dropped, and Milmo was able to tell the court:

> My clients would have welcomed a trial of these actions so that they could personally denounce what they can only regard as out-and-out lies, but in the circumstances feel that by this statement and the payments of very substantial damages, their reputations have been sufficiently vindicated.

One wonders why Dr Casey and Tregear accepted the settlement instead of pursuing the case. The end result was that the original *Eye* story was repeated in the national newspapers, to be read by millions of new readers. Of course, there were 'very large' damages payments, although the quantities involved were not disclosed in court. In fact, these amounted to a £22,000 – £15,000 to Dr Casey, £7,000 to Tregear. Given the facts of the case as outlined in the settlement statement by Milmo, Dr Casey and Tregear might have expected much more money – perhaps five times as much – had they won the case in court; and it seems likely that they would have done so. Since the burden of proof in libel cases is placed upon the defendant, *Private Eye* would have had to have proved that Dr Casey and Tregear had gone to bed together – which would presumably involve producing a witness who had been in the bedroom at the time of the alleged act.

So why did *Private Eye* consider seeking to fight this case on justification? Given that Ingrams believed that Dr Casey and Tregear had gone to bed together, was there a faint hope at the *Eye* that the plaintiffs would be frightened off? Ingrams' reasoning works something like this: if people have done something wrong, they will usually deny it. But they will be reluctant to lie in open court under the gaze of the national media.

The reputations of Dr Casey and Tregear were restored by the statement in court, and they had won not inconsiderable damages. *Private Eye* lost £22,000, plus costs, and had its reputation for scurrility confirmed yet again. On the face of it, Dr Casey and Tregear won and *Private Eye* lost. But in real life, as opposed to the law, matters are rather more complex.

Many readers of national newspapers will have formed the view that there is no smoke without fire – especially given Fleet Street's tendency to highlight the seamier aspects of a story, and the fact that no details were offered as to how *Private Eye* got the story and came to print it. What were these innocent readers told about *Private Eye*, other than that it was 'a satirical magazine', and that this was one of the most scurrilous items to have appeared in it? Few readers are likely to have supposed that *Eye* reporters conjured the story out of thin air. On the other hand if, say, five million newspaper readers saw the settlement report – a conservative estimate – it is surely no exaggeration to suppose that five hundred of them might have decided to take a look at *Private Eye* in the future. And if only two hundred of those then took out a subscription, their combined payments would equal the sum paid out to Dr Casey and Tregear.

Of course, this is only conjecture. But time after time *Private Eye* has shown that litigants who plunge into the morass of the libel laws seldom emerge either much better off financially or untainted by the original defamation. *Private Eye*, however, has proved itself remarkably resilient to losing in the courts.

In the Dr Casey affair, as in many others, the plaintiff's lawyer made free use of the word 'scurrilous'. It is an oddly equivocal word. Lawyers appear to think that it is deeply pejorative, and that anyone, or anything, so labelled will thereafter be deprived of public respect and confidence. Yet in popular usage it is a term almost of approbation. Fleet Street editors urge their diarists to become scurrilous, meaning lightheartedly bitchy. To most editors this is far preferable to the kind of personality sketches and straightforward reporting of social events which used to fill diaries, and which they now regard as toadying.

Private Eye had been both the pioneer and the chief beneficiary of the new public acceptance of disrespectful personal commentary. And the frequent description of the *Eye* as scurrilous must frequently have won the magazine new readers. The *Eye* has also consistently overturned the humbug of a legal system in which slippery twentieth-century citizens with a grievance are assumed to be eighteenth-century-style men of honour unless proved conclusively to be otherwise. The image of the wronged innocent is not an easy one to maintain in a court battle with *Private Eye*.

In the Dr Casey affair it would have been interesting to have had an explanation from Milmo of exactly how the careers and personal lives of his clients had been affected by the *Private Eye* story. He told Mr Justice Hutchinson that Dr Casey was a man 'of complete moral probity whose friendship with Mr Tregear is wholly normal and irreproachable'. There is no doubt that it was. But is 'complete moral probity' a prerequisite of a university lecturer today? And, outside a court of law, could Dr Casey ever describe himself in such terms and keep a straight face? Milmo's description of Dr Casey has provided the *Private Eye* card index with a useful quote in the unhappy event of Dr Casey falling short of this high standard.

What the court reports never touch upon is the curious and fascinating area of backstage settlement details. Indeed, included in some settlements is the provision that these details will not be disclosed. The sums paid out in damages are usually described as 'substantial', 'very substantial' or just 'a sum of money'. In the case of Dr Casey and Mr Tregear the agreement was that they should be described as 'very substantial'. Why not say exactly how much? Would the public, having read the details of this case and the indignant words of Milmo, have considered £22,000 'very substantial'?

At one time or another most of *Private Eye*'s enemies and targets have rationalised their hatred of the magazine by saying that they would not be so annoyed by it if only *Eye* reporters would just take the trouble to check the details with them. This always sounds very reasonable until you remember that *Private Eye* is not dealing with who won the tombola prize at the Young Farmers' Ball. If *Private Eye* has any *raison d'être* it is that the magazine sets out to print stories which are deemed unfit for the national press. Few uncontentious stories are printed in *Private Eye*; and all of its stories include details that the people and institutions concerned do not want to see in print. Such details cannot simply be checked by a quick phone call. The press as a whole is awash with inaccuracies. There is scarcely an article about or an interview with a leading public figure that is not inaccurate in some innocent detail. Naturally, no one complains when their achievements or qualities have been overstated, unless it has been done to such an extent as to make them sound ridiculous.

In 1986 the record shop tycoon Richard Branson was the subject of many fulsome articles in the press. No doubt these contained a number of exaggerations about his achievements. Branson – an old *Eye* enemy – had no complaint about that. However, when I wrote in the London *Standard* a few (I thought) mildly critical comments about him – only mild comments get past the paper's lawyers – the tycoon sent round an angry letter which was printed next day.

In my experience newspapers are increasingly gutless about questioning the motives and actions of rich men who make themselves known to, or are befriended by, starstruck proprietors. While writing the 'William Hickey' column I was upbraided by the then owner of the *Express* for describing Lord Forte as 'a former ice cream salesman'. Interference at this trivial level is unimportant, but it is symptomatic of a more pernicious and corrupt tendency in Fleet Street today. Michael Gillard left the *Express* to write the 'Slicker' column for the *Eye* because his former proprietor, Sir Max Aitken, received complaints from powerful business friends that Gillard was actually daring to do his job – which was to enquire into the affairs of important companies, including their own. *Private Eye* has now been battered by court cases for twenty-five years, and has made hundreds of enemies. But it has amassed a readership approaching one million which encompasses all social classes. By no means all of its readers can approve of all its contents. But it is fair to assume that most of them approve of most of it. If that is so, its friends by far outnumber its enemies.

Chapter Five

Enemies . . . And a Few Friends

Although *Private Eye* has probably received more writs for libel in its twenty-five years than most newspapers have in their considerably longer histories, not all who find themselves lampooned in its 'funnies' or exposed in its news or gossip sections have resorted to legal action. The *Eye* has always made a point of ridiculing political leaders, but they, knowing well how volatile the tide of public opinion can be, have generally been unwilling to test the strength of their reputations in a protracted legal battle with the merry band of satirists from Gnome House.

Rushton caricatured Harold Macmillan as an old tart during the Profumo affair – ogling horribly while sitting cross-legged and naked on a chair. But he did not sue for that, nor for countless other humiliations. At the same time the magazine carried four photographs of his deputy, Home Secretary Rab Butler, each with a caption. They read:

I admit the Immigration Bill ran counter to all my principles . . .
And I know that flogging lunatics in gaol doesn't do anybody any good . . .
Of course I shared everyone's doubts about Hanratty's sanity . . .
The fact remains – I'M JUST A FLABBY FACED OLD COWARD

Private Eye added two postscripts:

P.S. And what's more, he's such a flabby faced old coward he won't even sue us.

P.P.S. And even if he does sue us he's STILL a flabby faced old coward.

They were not sued. Macmillian's successor Sir Alec Douglas-Home was accused of killing a fellow pupil with a cricket stump while at Eton, and Willie Rushton was put up to stand against him in a by-election. *Private Eye* suggested they might arrange a citizen's arrest of the Prime Minister. Home believed that he was eventually laughed out of office, and he is probably right. The *Eye* also said that President John Kennedy, a Roman Catholic, had had a secret, earlier marriage and divorce that had been hushed up. They were not sued for that, either.

Harold Wilson, so far Britain's longest-serving Prime Minister since the war, served an equally long stretch in the pages of the *Eye*. Ingrams' view of Wilson was that the Labour leader was essentially a journalist at heart who had somehow strayed into high politics, accompanied by his long-suffering wife, Mary.

It was true that Wilson had been a distinguished journalist, adroit enough to manage the difficult task – for a future Labour politician – of composing leader page features for the ultra-Conservative *Sunday Express*. He had also been one of that paper's principal political informants in the 1950s; and while Prime Minister he was guest of honour at the *Sunday Express's* lavish fiftieth anniversary banquet at the Savoy Hotel in the 1960s. He delivered a delightfully funny speech, cleverly structured in the 'As he taps his lightly boiled brown egg this morning . . .' style of the paper's 'Crossbencher' column, to which he had been an anonymous contributor. This little-known aspect of Wilson's history fascinated Ingrams, and although it might have been hard for the Labour leader to appreciate it in the face of ferocious later attacks, it tended to soften the *Eye's* attitude to 'Wislon' personally.

For years Ingrams was convinced that Wilson's position was weakened by his reliance on rich, self-interested men who professed to share his mixed-economy socialist ideas. He was particularly suspicious of those of East European origin, such as the Yorkshire textile magnate Joe Kagan, who was known to have had links with the Soviet KGB and with Rudy Sternberg, whose business affairs often took him behind the Iron Curtain. Wilson gave peerages to both Kagan and Sternberg.

Wilson could claim rightly that these men had made a success of their lives in Britain, had become fully integrated into our way of life, and while not patriots in the fullest sense – they had not fought for this country in a war – they had created employment for thousands of citizens. So what if Kagan had had contacts with Russia's intelligence systems, or if Sternberg – also suspected of having such connections – travelled to and from the Soviet Union? Wilson, too, as a consultant for the London timber company Montague Meyer, had made business trips to Russia while Labour was in opposition in the 1950s.

Ingrams was also fascinated by the relationship between Harold Wilson and his secretary, Marcia Williams – whom Wilson also sent eventually to the House of Lords. An early feature of the *Eye* spoof 'Mrs Wilson's Diary' was its portrayal of Marcia as all-powerful in the Wilson kitchen cabinet. If anything, this portrayal of Marcia was comically understated. It emerged that she had composed an honours list (on lavender writing paper), and that she had had red dispatch boxes delivered to the home she shared with the then political editor of the *Daily Mail*, Walter Terry, by whom she had two illegitimate children. Mrs Williams also figured in what became known as the 'Slagheap Affair' in which, with various other members of her family, she conducted the negotiations for a controversial land deal from Wilson's office.

Private Eye was supplied constantly with anonymous information about Wilson and his life since the 1940s, which Marnham suggested was sent to the *Eye* by the British intelligence services. Wilson himself believed he was being bugged by MI5. This was perhaps not surprising as it later transpired that Kagan, in and out of Number Ten regularly, had maintained his friendship with a Russian he had met during the Soviet invasion of Lithuania – the same man who was KGB chief in London during Wilson's occupation of Number Ten.

Nearly all of the business men who befriended Wilson had their affairs exposed by *Private Eye*. Paul Foot wrote a long article detailing the activities of Wilson cronies, in particular their trading links with the Soviet Union and Israel. He also made a point of pursuing stories about tensions and disagreements between members of Wilson's Downing Street entourage.

Those Wilson sent to the Lords – including Lady Falkender – played no further role in politics, and Wilson himself retreated into obscurity after his surprise and virtually unexplained resignation in 1976. Although he was made a Knight of the Garter by the Queen, who was said to have been fond of him, and became a life peer, he failed to emerge as an elder statesman whose counsel was sought by his successors.

His administration had been attacked ceaselessly by the mainly Tory press, but *Private Eye* had scored by far the most direct hits; and 'Mrs Wilson's Diary' had proved to be remarkably prescient in its descriptions of Marcia's role in Wilson's life.

The noble Lady Falkender contributed nothing to the debates in the House of Lords, but her title appeared in the 1980s above a political column in the *Mail on Sunday*, owned by the Conservative Associated Newspapers. Some thought it odd that this woman with so many secrets, and so much to reveal herself about her political years, should be paid by a Tory group to put her name on a ghost-written column of trivial Commons gossip.

Ingrams was told from time to time that Marcia would like to come to a *Private Eye* lunch, but he was not interested. She had been an enemy, and she would remain one. Similar approaches were made by Sir John Junor on behalf of Tory politician Reginald Maudling, whose slippery business connections had been exposed in the *Eye*. Junor suggested that he bring the Tory Home Secretary to a lunch with Ingrams – 'and you'll see he's a very nice man'. Ingrams refused. He told me: 'There's no point. He might well be a very nice man, but he's a crook.'

Jeremy Thorpe was the subject of one of *Private Eye*'s most violently vulgar covers when, in 1979, he was acquitted at the Old Bailey of conspiring to murder a homosexual man who had sought to blackmail him. The cover showed a photograph taken of Mr Thorpe with his second wife, Marion; both are smiling and Thorpe is waving his hat. The headline read: 'Grand Acquittal Souvenir'. The caption bubbles had Thorpe saying 'Buggers can't be losers', while Marion comments: 'You lucky sod!'

There had been anger and depression at *Private Eye* when Thorpe was acquitted. But Ingrams was all smiles. 'It means we can go on attacking him.' In fact, when Thorpe retired from public life the *Eye* lost interest in him.

They had pursued the story far harder than any Fleet Street paper, with the aid of a most unlikely ally – the police. *Private Eye* has never been a particular supporter of the police (or of anyone else). But in the Thorpe case one of their most powerful articles, 'The Ditto Man', was compiled from the transcripts of police interviews with the Liberal leader. Thorpe refused to answer question after question, but repeatedly replied, 'Ditto.' Police on the case thought there was the basis for a charge, but it took some time to convince the Director of Public Prosecutions that proceedings should be taken against him. The same had happened in the case of former diplomat Sir Peter Heyman, whom the *Eye* exposed as having taken part in child pornography. Patrick Marnham commented in his book:

> . . . it is an interesting sidelight thrown by the Thorpe and Heyman stories that in order for one section of the state's prosecutors to get around another it had to circumvent the national press, which was itself considered too establishment-minded to work the trick.

A bizarre feature of the Thorpe case was the intervention of Harold Wilson, who offered the view that South African intelligence agents, of all people, had been behind the exposure of the Liberal leader. Given the full (if anonymous) assistance of senior police officials in the case, the suggestion that South African agents might have been involved smacked of paranoia, if not downright lunacy. Ingrams was thoroughly intrigued by the thought of the ex-Prime Minister brooding over the case and coming up with the unexpected idea of BOSS agents fishing in the curious backwaters of Thorpe's life.

Thorpe was lampooned in the 'funnies' and exposed in the news sections. And on this occasion there was a further contribution which fell somewhere between the two – Auberon Waugh took a deep interest in the whole murky affair. He attended the various court hearings, wrote a book about the case, and stood against Thorpe in a by-election. With the *Eye*'s support, Waugh set himself up as the candidate for the Dog Lover's Party. (In the course of Thorpe's long dispute with the homosexual male model Norman Scott, an incident on Exmoor took place, during which Scott's dog, Rinka, was shot dead.) A large dog was hired from an agency, and Bron posed with it in Soho Square for his election posters. Early on in the affair, Waugh had the pleasure of describing the case to Thorpe's predecessor as Liberal leader, Jo Grimond. He came to an *Eye* luncheon, where it was revealed that he knew nothing whatsoever of the story. Bron was delighted to witness Grimond's huge amusement and amazement as he was filled in on all the details.

Private Eye found a new lawyer to hate in the Thorpe case – Sir David Napley, Thorpe's solicitor; and a new judge to be lampooned, Mr Justice Cantley, whose direction to the jury in the case was widely considered to have left no doubt about Thorpe's innocence. He was billed thereafter as 'Cocklecantly', after the lamentably ill-informed Judge Cocklecarrot in the old 'Beachcomber' column.

There was some talk early in the *Eye*'s campaign of

Thorpe bringing a case of criminal libel, and even that this might be financed by Sir James Goldsmith. Certainly some of Thorpe's friends were urging this course. But nothing came of it. *Private Eye* was not like a newspaper which could be sued into silence, since its editorial and business affairs were run by the same man, Ingrams. It was not unrealistic to believe that he would run the magazine into the ground rather than give up on a story; and even if that happened, what was to stop Ingrams starting it up all over again on his release from prison? Thorpe, like Wilson, had led a complex and varied life, and had had to overcome many obstacles on his way to public prominence. Inevitably, perhaps, he had also made enemies, but it is fair to speculate that he had met nothing like *Private Eye*, or Ingrams, before.

When *Private Eye* took up the cudgels it was never less than brutally tenacious; and as it took up position in the front line, old antagonists of its victims would line up behind to keep the supply lines of information open. Both Wilson's administration and Thorpe's personal affairs were exposed by insiders, who knew that their knowledge would find a ready market at the *Eye*. Goldsmith was undermined by City businessmen who had crossed swords with him in the past. In all cases *Private Eye* also received help from Fleet Street journalists and editors. By running its campaigns openly in the pages of the magazine, *Private Eye* has always received support from unexpected quarters.

The critic Clive James, himself an *Eye* target, coined a neat description of the *Eye* as the magazine 'that sends children home crying from school'. Ingrams, and Waugh, have little truck with this view, holding that it is the behaviour of the parents which causes the distress in the first place. Waugh adds that, in any case, what is so terrible about the kiddies crying? Kiddies cry all the time. Was he to be impeded by the blubbing of brats whose parents had had rude things said about them? Besides which, an appearance in *Private Eye*, though usually derogatory, is not always considered such a bad thing. A not inconsiderable group of people wear their scars with pride, heeding the consolation of friends who point out that to be attacked in the *Eye* is to have finally arrived on the vaudeville stage that it has created out of British life.

Anthony Haden-Guest is an amusing example of this reaction. An excitable, noisy author of occasional articles for colour supplement magazines, and by no means a major figure even in the shallows of Fleet Street, his possibilities as a *Private Eye* stock character were first identified by Nigel Dempster. There followed a stream of 'Grovel' stories about Haden-Guest's extravagant behaviour at London social events, and he was nicknamed 'The Beast'.

Ingrams loved the image of Haden-Guest as a man who, according to Dempster's flights of fancy, had merely to appear in an upper-class drawing room for a social occasion to degenerate into chaos. Ingrams saw in Haden-Guest elements of Captain Foulenough, a character from the satirical writings of H. B. Morton, who wrote the 'Beachcomber' column in the *Daily Express* for nearly fifty years.

The notoriety Haden-Guest achieved through the 'Grovel' column was envied by many of his friends. Far from being debarred from social events, he became, if anything, more sought after. It is also fair to suggest that, like Denis Thatcher, to an extent he grew into the caricature of himself so lovingly created by Dempster.

But he liked to complain that he was sick and tired of being the butt of *Private Eye* jokes, and on one memorable occasion he was provided with an excellent opportunity for doing so. A team from BBC TV were filming a *Private Eye* luncheon to which Haden-Guest had been invited. At the top of his considerable voice, Haden-Guest announced: '*Private Eye* has ruined my life.' His declaration was greeted by one and all, and eventually even by himself, with loud and prolonged laughter.

In time he moved to New York, where he also developed a lively reputation on the social scene. But he always kept in touch with Dempster, his old tormentor. One night he joined Dempster, myself and the then *Daily Express* New

York correspondent Brian Vine at a smart Manhattan restaurant, where he symbolically punished 'Grovel' for the past indiscretions.

Before the aghast eyes of American diners, he threw Dempster over his knee and spanked Nigel to the accompaniment of Brian Vine cracking a spoon on the neck of a champagne bottle. Later they danced together. Few *Private Eye* victims have been able to exact their revenge in so direct a fashion, far less bury their emnity on the dance floor immediately afterwards.

Ingrams is insulated from most of his enemies because he is not a social man. He returns each evening of the on week to Aldworth. On the rare occasions when he stays up in town – at his mother's home in Chelsea – it is usually to go to a concert with Paul Foot. He has never been part of any London dinner party circuit. Nor is he usually invited to society occasions where he might meet those he attacks.

But in 1986 he was photographed at a Foyle's literary luncheon with the Archbishop of Canterbury, Robert Runcie, a frequent *Eye* target whom Ingrams considers 'useless' because 'he never says what he means'. The Archbishop's wife, Rosalind Runcie, says of *Private Eye*:

> I used to be amused by *Private Eye* and laughed and laughed at one particular picture, and then laughed again when I thought about it. But the magazine has stopped being funny now. It hasn't damaged us because we don't really take any notice of it – though I was intrigued by the fact that Auberon Waugh kept writing about me, about coming to see me, inviting me out to meals and so on. To be fair he always said I'd refused his invitations. But I have never spoken to him in my life, and I thought: 'Why does he keep writing this about me?' That puzzled me.

One annual event at which he is always exposed to enemies is the *Spectator* magazine's summer party. Here, Ingrams deploys a kind of reverse snobbery, and boasts about the prominent men and women who have cut him dead. Of course, he is a star at such occasions. Ingrams has what an aristocratic Scottish friend of mind defines as a 'difficult-to-know' charisma. He makes no effort to approach anyone. If someone he has not been introduced to approaches him he is bleak to the point of rudeness, especially if it is evident that they have been drinking.

Feuds with *Private Eye*, and Ingrams, are usually for all time; in Fleet Street that is rarely the case. Jocelyn Stevens feuded with the *Eye* and Ingrams for years. At one time we were colleagues on the *Daily Express*, and some tactful soul asked Jocelyn if it was right and proper that we should be seen together. Stevens replied that it was fine by him. He made so many new enemies that from time to time he had to make room for them in his demonology by reprieving old ones.

Ingrams has reached an enviable position as editor of *Private Eye*. Malcolm Muggeridge has cited it as the chief reason for being a journalist: 'You don't have to like anyone.' Ingrams also delighted in an old Enoch Powell maxim: 'If you are against everything, sooner or later you will be proved right.'

An indication of how little some people mind about being teased in *Private Eye* is given by the fact that many of them are eager to meet Ingrams and the *Eye* staff. Erin Pizzey (the 'Chiswick Lard Mountain' who gave her first husband such a mauling in the divorce courts that he might have qualified for a place in a battered husbands' hostel, had such a place existed) was once invited by Auberon Waugh to an *Eye* lunch with her second husband. Clearly the memory of the *Eye* reports on the case had faded. There was only one problem: Ingrams had not been consulted, and he did not approve. Before the lunch began he changed around the placement cards so that Bron had to sit at one end of the long table with the Pizzeys, while Ingrams sat at the other end and ignored the guests throughout the meal. He chuckled afterwards about Waugh's fury.

Some *Eye* enemies come in pairs. The Shrimsley brothers are one example. The journalist Alan Brien had been an *Eye* stalwart in the 1960s, but when in 1973 he became the third husband of feminist writer Jill Tweedie, and wrote a book about women's breasts, he was teased regularly. In time, Brien and Tweedie faded from the *Eye* gallery of stock joke characters. Ms Tweedie says now: 'I think I regard *Private Eye* really as a species of spider. You know, it's very interesting and one looks at it, but with a certain repulsion. At the beginning I used to be a bit hurt by it. Later on I found I was rather hurt when they left me out.'

Desmond Wilcox and Esther Rantzen effortlessly became the *Eye*'s most hated couple. Rantzen began her TV career as an assistant to Bernard Braden, an original shareholder in the *Eye*. Soon, Braden was sacked by the BBC and replaced by Rantzen. Wilcox left his wife Patsy to move in with Rantzen, and later he married her. *Private Eye* drew attention to their activities, in particular the perks Miss Rantzen enjoyed in her new job, and the royalties Wilcox earned from books taken in part from transcripts of programmes he worked on.

There were good reasons for highlighting the careers of Rantzen and Wilcox inside a public corporation. But there was also a puritanical element in Ingrams' campaign against them. As far as he was concerned, Esther Rantzen had broken up a marriage, and Wilcox was a pathetic middle-aged man who had ditched his wife for a young floozie.

But Ingrams was no more consistent in this respect than he is in many others. His best friend Paul Foot had married twice, although he got around this in *Who's Who* by stating simply that he was married and had three sons. Booker has married three times, and was equally coy when it came to filling in the *Who's Who* forms. Ingrams noted the omissions and saw them as hypocrisy, but it did not affect his friendship with them.

Another sure way onto the Ingrams hit list is to call *Private Eye* names. *Daily Mail* editor Sir David English confirmed his permanent position in this select group by referring to an *Eye* article about his paper as 'a festering lie'. Years later, long after even the most devout readers would have forgotten the original row, he was referred to as 'Sir David Fester'.

English has never sued *Private Eye* for any of its attacks, but he has used his newspaper, when appropriate, to hit back. In 1986, after Tory backbencher Sir Frederic Bennett had won £25,000 in damages from the *Eye*, the *Daily Mail* ran a prominent story next day headlined 'Tory knight named as *Private Eye*'s "mole" in MP's libel action'. The article was effusively flattering about Sir Frederic and his travails with the 'scurrilous' magazine. The information on Sir Frederic had been supplied to the *Eye* anonymously by Sir Richard Body, a fellow Tory MP and formerly 'Old Muckspreader'. The *Mail* commented: 'The magazine has a dubious reputation for "shopping" its contacts and contributors when the legal going has got rough.' This was seen by Ingrams as a reference to the case of Cecil Parkinson and Nigel Dempster, and he angrily wrote an account of that case in the next issue, putting the blame firmly on Dempster.

But the *Private Eye*–English feud dated back to a far more intriguing skirmish which involved the Queen. During the Yorkshire Ripper case the *Eye* reported that *Mail* executives were entertaining members of the Ripper's family in the north while preparing a background report on the case; the *Eye* suggested that the *Mail* men had promised to pay large sums of money for the exclusive co-operation of the Ripper's family. The mother of one of the girls murdered by the Ripper then wrote to the Queen drawing attention to the *Eye* story, and received a sympathetic reply. This made the front page of several newspapers. The *Mail* responded with a huge article, masterminded by Sir David English, entitled 'Anatomy of a Festering Lie'. The *Eye* story, supplied by a local freelance journalist who had witnessed the *Mail* men in action, was partly true. The *Mail* did not pay out a huge sum, but it did entertain relatives, and had paid money for exclusive information.

Sir David English and Ingrams could never have been friends, but their attitudes and methods often seemed similar: both enjoyed a kind of tyranny over their employees; both delighted in gossip and mischief; both were puritanical – in his middle age English joined Ingrams in disapproving strongly of adultery, and he too became religious. Both were also obsessional, and their papers often reflected their obsessions. Ingrams battered away at enemies long after they had sunk over the horizon; so did English whose *bête noir* was the 'rival' (the *Mail* always put quote marks around the word) *Daily Express*. I was often reminded of Captain Ahab and his pursuit of Moby Dick by English's eternal quest to harpoon the great, ageing beast which lay on the other side of *Fleet Street*. No matter what depths it plumbed to evade his spear, the *Mail*, with English on the bridge, would follow. Executives who left or were pitched overboard by the *Express* were picked up by English and grilled about their knowledge of the beast's workings.

But English was a canny realist as far as the *Eye* was concerned. He could live with it, and even profit by it. For years he turned a blind eye to Dempster's activities as 'Grovel' because the 'rival' *Daily Express* management was often a prime target of the column. He chortled at the *Eye*'s *Express* nicknames – the *Getsworse*, the *Getsmuchworse* and, for a short time, the *Daily Tits-by-Christmas*.

English is certainly a doughty opponent, especially when one considers the vast gulf that separates a newspaper like the *Mail* from *Private Eye*. Ingrams has never cared much about reader reaction, and certainly he has never refrained from publishing repeated attacks and endless jokes about public figures for fear of producing the counter-productive effect of enlisting sympathy for the victim. A joke only becomes boring when he decides it is – though to be fair he has usually been content to allow readers to express their tedium in the letters pages. English cannot allow himself the luxury of this point of view, and would be hard put to maintain a permanent campaign against the *Eye* in the pages of the *Daily Mail*.

Most of the *Eye*'s enemies are reluctant to talk publicly about

Ingrams or his magazine. Harold Wilson once castigated it in the House of Commons, but he is chary of doing so outside. Mary Wilson told *Woman's Own* that she would like to bite John Wells, co-creator of 'Mrs Wilson's Diary'. The disgraced former Labour MP John Stonehouse, who provided many laughs for *Eye* readers, sounded rather confused in his comments for this book:

> I think *Private Eye* is scurrilous – or was. It has harmed a lot of decent people who didn't deserve what they got. It has exaggerated obscenely about certain events. It has traded in titillation for people who never made or even attempted to make a decent contribution to society. My comments are purely historical because in recent years it has become extremely boring and I only read it occasionally, when I am more than ever bored by it. I think the only reason it had a following some years ago was that it was prepared to make libellous statements for which it, of course, paid large amounts of money. Now that it can no longer afford to take that risk it has become boring. I am not amused by it. I am bored. The only good thing about it at one time were its amusing covers. I don't know who was responsible for those but they were slightly amusing.

Lord Grade is more generous:

> I buy it every time it comes out, every issue. And I enjoy it thoroughly. So does my wife. I read the newspapers first and then when I want to be amused I read *Private Eye*, usually in the evening when I get home from the office. Hurt by it? No. They've called me 'Low Greed'. But it's better than being called 'High Greed', isn't it?

It would be misleading to suppose that everyone in public life fears and dislikes *Private Eye*. It has friends in high places as well as low – people as diverse as the old woman who wrote in to say she would have been dead by now if she hadn't discovered her fortnightly tonic, and the eminent Master of the Rolls, Lord Denning, of whom Ingrams wrote in *Goldenballs*:

Since his appointment as Master of the Rolls in 1962, Lord Denning has gained a reputation among journalists as a judge who, unlike almost all his fellows, does really believe in the freedom of the press. Time and again in cases involving newspapers, Denning has over-ruled the decisions of lower courts to the advantage of newspapers. Such an attitude in a British judge is extremely rare. Our judges, on the whole, regard the press as a nuisance and a threat to their own authority . . .

Denning was the only judge in the course of the Goldsmith case who was wholeheartedly in favour of *Private Eye*'s side . . . whereas Judge Wien, for example, had taken the view that Goldsmith was a pillar of society, Denning's remarks throughout implied that he did not think too much either of him or his lawyer Levine. The key word in his vocabulary was 'respectable' . . . [Our] distributors were all respectable firms – wholesalers and retailers 'of good standing' . . . Goldsmith and Levine were not so described.

Here is the Ingrams' romanticism at work. He describes Denning as 'ruddy faced' . . . looking and speaking 'like an old Hampshire farmer':

His pleasant rustic voice struck a delightfully incongruous note in the heavy court atmosphere.

Ingrams is a devoted reader of the nineteenth-century farmer and pamphleteer William Cobbett, who was jailed for two years for criminal libel in 1809. He saw in Denning's rural Hampshire common sense echoes of Cobbett, and he spared no effort to let the old judge know that he had won over the pamphleteers at *Private Eye*. It was a proud moment for Ingrams when he was photographed with Denning at a social occasion in 1986.

Another legal luminary in the Goldsmith case became a friend of the *Eye* and Ingrams – James Comyn, QC, who later became Judge Comyn. He too was a rustic figure, a kind of Irish Rumpole.

Ingrams describes their first meeting:

He was a small, stooping, bespectacled Irishman, rather

shabbily dressed, his trousers frayed, his cuffs white with the ash of Sweet Aftons which he chain smoked. His room in Queen Elizabeth Building with its high windows looking out over the Embankment was in a state of Dickensian chaos. Bundles of briefs and law books lay all over the floor. There was what looked like a bottle of eggnog under a table.

Ingrams was enchanted by Comyn, whose office sounded very similar to the editor's eyrie at *Private Eye* – sans eggnog and Sweet Aftons, of course. Comyn's subsequent confrontation with Goldsmith during the prelude to the criminal libel case deepened Ingrams' admiration for the Irish Rumpole. For the first time during the committal proceedings, Goldsmith appeared with his mistress, Lady Annabel Birley, and the court was packed with press and spectators, although the case was little more than a formality. Ingrams' own account of this event shows his developing love affair with Comyn:

It was very diverting. James Comyn, asking questions in his soft Irish voice, managed to provoke [Goldsmith] almost to a frenzy. As he paced up and down the narrow witness box, like one of Aspinall's tigers, his voice rose to a high pitch and he spat out his words with contempt. The idea of the Lucan circle was 'a total nonsense and fabrication'. What did he think of the Elwes part of the story, which he hadn't sued over?
'I regard it as the typical filth of this magazine.'
'Isn't it your aim to smash *Private Eye*?' Comyn asked quietly.
'No,' Goldsmith snarled, leaning across and jabbing his finger at me, 'I only want them to be more TRUTHFUL!'
'Do you mind behaving a little less theatrically, Sir James?' the magistrate, Mr Kenneth Barraclough, asked. Afterwards, Annabel Birley could be heard congratulating [Goldsmith] 'You were F. E. Smith reincarnated,' she said, and Aspinall added loyally: 'I think we got them with both barrels.'

Comyn kept in touch with Ingrams and *Private Eye* after he retired. Ingrams believed that the evident support of Denning and the quirky Irish needling of Comyn in the preliminary cases weakened the resolve of Goldsmith and his supporters, and in the end led to the settlement of all the cases.

Rowland 'Tiny' Rowland might have seemed a natural supporter of Goldsmith, in that he, like Goldsmith, had German origins and had worked his way up from humble beginnings to become a multi-millionaire. But he sent £5,000 to the Goldenballs Fund, by far the largest contribution. It emerged that Goldsmith and Rowland were not friends.

Ingrams spoke to Rowland at the time, and asked him how much support he would give: 'The sky's the limit,' Rowland replied. Ingrams said later: 'Tiny was adamant that there would be no *quid pro quo*, and no question of laying off him in the future.' Rowland had also been the subject of many *Private Eye* attacks, and these continued after the Goldsmith case.

One of the *Eye*'s earliest supporters was the Eighth Earl of Arran, who wrote a column for the London *Evening News*. Neither 'Boofy' nor the *Evening News* are with us any more. Arran wrote a sprightly weekly piece for the *News*, remembered chiefly for its eccentricity. He became famous in Switzerland for writing that the Swiss as a race were 'smelly' because of their reluctance to open windows. But he had nothing but praise for the *Eye*.

I am going on about *Private Eye*. Buy it. It is the best informed, perhaps most important publication of the era. I mean exactly what I say. Historians will read it as an accurate reflection of the times long after they have given up *The Times* itself which represents nobody and nothing, just like Trog Smog [William Rees Mogg] the editor himself. The *Economist* and the *Spectator* may reflect financial and political trends, but the pattern of society itself is to be traced in the satirical pages of *Private Eye*. I do not believe that is the intention, but it is what is being achieved. Personally I now rate *Private Eye* high enough to think it should be represented in the Press Gallery. No doubt this idea will infuriate the lobby correspondents who carry on like little tin gods and whose judgement as to what is important is almost invariably faulty.

This cutting from Arran's column of 1 July 1970 is marked '1st Edition *Evening News*', which suggests that his stirring support for the *Eye* did not survive the editor's first perusal. Boofy was not taken very seriously, but he did have an influence on the *Eye* in the early days. The fight to get the magazine represented in the Press Gallery – by Auberon Waugh – was resisted by most of the newspaper correspondents there, as well as the Sergeant at Arms.

Arran's most spirited intervention in London's social life came in the 1970s, when his proprietor, Vere Harmsworth, tried to join the Beefsteak private luncheon club. He was seconded by Lords Hartwell and Cromer, but for a time his membership was blocked by the *Eye* enemy Paul Johnson and Tory MP Hugh Fraser, who said that no man who employed Nigel Dempster was fit to take his place among so distinguished a gathering.

Dempster had earned this opprobrium by writing about Johnson's friend Lady Antonia Fraser, who had just parted from Fraser. In 'Grovel' and in the *Daily Mail* Dempster detailed the love life of the 'much loved' lady historian, whose society was sought by a number of prominent men. (Clive James, reported 'Grovel', had been dismissed by Antonia, who told him: 'I only sleep with the First Eleven.')

Arran wrote to the Beefsteak's most senior member, the Duke of Devonshire, pleading the case for Vere and mentioning Johnson's animus against Dempster. This letter found its way into the pages of *Private Eye*:

My Dear Andrew,

I find myself in a highly embarrassing situation. I have heard in the last few days that there are people who want me to withdraw Vere Harmsworth's name as a candidate for election to the Beefsteak Club. I think you know something about this. Perhaps you can advise me.

I thought that as Esmond's son he would be welcome, more especially because his seconders are Rowley Cromer and

Michael Hartwell. On the contrary I hear he has enemies. More particularly I am told that Fearless Fraser has objected because of the vicious attacks by the odious Dempster on Antonia. Moreover, Paul Johnson has ganged up with Hugh because he is a friend of both Hugh and Antonia (I don't know how this can be, but he is).

The pathetic thing is that Vere, when looking for a seconder, picked on Paul Johnson, whom he described as a friend of his!

What do you think I should do – apart from leaving the country? Frankly the thought of telling Vere (and of course Esmond) appalls me. As does also the thought that I myself will have to resign, as I think your father did from the Turf when the late Lord Bearsted was pilled.

I do not think the club would mind that much if I resigned, though it is now my only club, and I normally have luncheon there every day. Indeed, it would be like saying goodbye to a friend.

Can I think that you might bring your considerable influence – I do not flatter you – to bear on the situation? I don't think that either Rowley or Michael cut much ice, though they too would find themselves in an embarrassing situation.

This is a real cri de coeur.

Harmsworth was admitted finally to the Beefsteak, and Dempster, far from being damaged by Johnson, flourished at the *Daily Mail*.

It is known that several copies of *Private Eye* are bought by the Royal household, and that Captain Mark Phillips is on the subscription list, as is the famous traitor Kim Philby. The wartime fighter ace Douglas Bader was a supporter of *Private Eye*, and the Earl of Arran used to plug it in his eccentric *Evening News* column. TV arts presenter Melvyn Bragg – 'Barg' in *Private Eye* lampoons – has been an avid supporter for years, as has Graham Greene, the only man to whom I have seen Ingrams visibly defer. Margaret Thatcher is an *Eye* reader, and was once taken to a fortnightly luncheon by Paul Foot. John Mortimer, the QC and author of the *Rumpole* books, has remained a close friend of Ingrams, even after Auberon Waugh once suggested in print that he should be offered the *Eye* brief in the Goldsmith litigation, 'because the booby might even believe in the case'. Jilly Cooper has been a supporter for years, despite *Eye* lampooning of her publisher husband Leo.

Lady Olga Maitland, the *Sunday Express* diarist, has helped the *Eye* with stories for years, often at the cost of friendship with her own proprietor. She has become a stock character in 'Grovel', usually offering controversial aristocratic views on topics of the day. Ingrams treasured one of her 1970s pronouncements about Prince Charles, which he said was most prescient: 'Mark my words, there's something wrong with that boy.'

The Old Etonian racing figure Charles Benson has been a willing anonymous contributor to 'Grovel', and also to the 'Colonel Mad' column even though his great patron, the Aga Khan, has on several occasions been voted 'Shit of the year'. Benson perhaps escaped suspicion, since from time to time he has been characterised as a sponger. The Greek playboy Taki Theadoracopoulos was a keen informant until Ingrams decided he was a 'glue-sniffing plagiarist'. Taki threatened once or twice to visit the Ingrams' manse armed with a baseball bat, but he settled instead for cutting Lord Gnome dead at the *Spectator*'s 1986 summer party.

Peter Jay has remained a close friend of *Private Eye*, despite constant belittlement in its pages after he accepted the post of Ambassador to Washington. The son-in-law of the Labour Prime Minister James Callaghan, he was chosen by Foreign Secretary David Owen – a friend – to replace senior diplomat Peter Ramsbotham. Thereafter he was 'Jaybotham' to Ingrams and *Private Eye*.

During the Goldsmith affair, Jay sent a cheque for £50 to the Goldenballs Fund, enclosing with it a little verse in Latin: *'Vivat Oculus, delendi sunt testes aurei'* ('Long live the *Eye*, the balls of gold must be destroyed'). Ingrams, it always seemed to me, was a little cold-hearted about Jay, who never complained about being insulted regularly in the *Eye*.

After returning from Washington, where his marriage had foundered, Jay presided over the disastrous launch of

TV-am. Afterwards he seemed rather ill-used and out of sorts. The Washington Ambassadorship should have brought a knighthood, but he never got one for reasons that are not clear. Ingrams saw him regularly, and Jay would offer advice and information. But Ingrams always seemed determined to punish Jay for having taken the Washington job, which he saw as an example of a good man being seduced by the trappings of power. In late summer of 1986, while we were composing a 'Sir Jonah Junor' column, Ingrams insisted on including a Jay item. It had just been announced that Jay had joined Robert 'Captain Bob' Maxwell as a consultant. What exactly was Jay going to consult about, Ingrams asked me. I had no idea, but said that *Mirror* friends had told me it was likely that the former ambassador might well be put in charge of their garage following a new edict from Captain Bob about which executives had a right to park there.

This did not fit in with what we thought 'Sir Jonah' would write – he would see a more sinister purpose behind the new partnership. So we decided on a typical 'Jonah' scheme of things, and suggested that Maxwell's unknown foreign backers, 'wherever they may reside', wanted Jay to provide an entrée for Czech-born Maxwell to the 'gilded salon doors' of high society. The obscure point was rammed home in the final paragraph, in which 'Sir Jonah' remarks: 'Small wonder I hold my nose as I pass the *Mirror* gulag in Holborn Circus.'

It was not a great Jonah item, but Ingrams liked it. If he could not find out what Jay was doing and print it in 'Grovel' or the news sections, then he was happy to speculate in the funnies. Jay took it all in good part, but Maxwell, then in litigation with *Private Eye*, is unlikely to have found the item very amusing. Still, Jay is a regular at *Eye* cricket matches, and is often accompanied by his children.

Sir John Junor's support of *Private Eye* has remained constant over the years. He has worked for three different *Sunday Express* proprietors, but to his credit he has never sought to disown *Private Eye* when the going got rough. In the days when his paper was owned by the Aitken family, *Private Eye* regularly ran stories about Sir Max, whom they called 'Biggles', and senior executives like John Coote – 'Captain John Coote RN (submerged)', so called because he commanded submarines during the course of his naval career.

Junor is a fascinating, quirky character, who has ploughed his own furrow through the higher echelons of political life, yet still manages to slum it up in Soho. He might spend the weekend with Margaret Thatcher at Chequers, and then have lunch with Ingrams on the following Tuesday. He never, to my knowledge, ever gave any information to *Private Eye* that we did not already possess in some form. But Ingrams always felt an affinity with Junor.

Private Eye once sailed into the *Daily Express*'s managing director Jocelyn Stevens – who was said to have become so angry in one previous job that he literally bit the carpet. Stevens knew that Junor was friendly with Ingrams, but he also realised that Junor had the upper hand in the *Express* group. For years the staid *Sunday Express* of Junor has kept the *Daily Express* afloat while successive editors, hired and fired by Jocelyn, have chopped and changed the failing daily.

Like Ingrams, Junor has no patience with long 'on the one hand . . . on the other hand' articles. If a Minister, in his judgement is not performing in a satisfactory manner, Junor's pithy leader column will say: 'Sack him.' Ingrams is fascinated by what will happen to the *Sunday Express* when Junor retires. Practically every time we met in 1986 he would ask me the latest on Junor's position. It became clear to me that he saw a parallel with his own position. He felt that the *Sunday Express* would collapse without Junor because Junor's personality was stamped on every page of the paper.

That is the position at *Private Eye*, too. Ian Hislop has assimilated many of Ingrams' attitudes, and he can think up jokes, but he would never pretend that he has Ingrams' authority. Ingrams, like Junor, has brought about this situation by failing to bring on people as the time for his retirement approaches. There are a handful of people on the *Sunday Express* who might be able to run the paper as a facsimile of the Junor model. But there are no young men in the wings ready to take the paper beyond Junor, building on its solid readership base. It is the same at *Private Eye*. Ingrams and Junor are men who do everything. Neither of them, by design, has instituted a proper hierarchy that will continue to function when they leave.

They make an odd pair at lunch. Junor is a serious gossip, who all but sets an agenda for the topics that are to be covered. Ingrams is not quite so formal; but he, too, has little time for theoretical or philosophical conversation. Both like to be in control. Junor's method of seizing the conversational initiative is to launch into a series of fulsome compliments to his guests, a useful method of getting their attention. I recall an occasion when he invited Nigel Dempster, Peter Tory of the *Star* and myself to lunch. He arranged the drinks, shooed the waiters away, and began: 'Now Peter [to me] you will be editor of the *Sunday Express*; Nigel, you must become editor of the *Daily Mail* . . .' There was a brief, respectful silence as this information sank in. Then Junor noticed that he had not given an exalted position to Peter Tory. 'And you Peter – you're the finest writer of us all.'

He fixes up his lunches with Ingrams weeks in advance. In addition, if one of his lunch dates falls through at the last moment, he will often ring Ingrams in the hope that he will be free.

One day, during the time when Trafalgar House owned the *Daily Express* – and at a time when the *Eye* was assailing its proprietor, Victor Matthews, with various business allegations – Junor rang Ingrams and said he wanted to fix a lunch quickly.

'I have to see you, Richard, it's important – I want to talk to you about Victor.'

Ingrams agreed, thinking that for once Junor was going

to come through with some usable information. After the usual, fussy Junor preliminaries with waiters – Junor is a most considerate host – he fixed Ingrams with his hooded, blue eyes, paused in theatrical fashion, lowered his voice and said: 'Richard, I have something to tell you about Victor Matthews. He is not a Jew.' Ingrams loves this story and was tickled by the urgency with which it was told. He could never find out why Junor thought he, Ingrams, believed Matthews was a Jew, nor why, if he wasn't, Junor supposed this would radically transform *Private Eye*'s attitude towards the building tycoon. It never changed, and was dictated by Matthews' decision to start a paper, the *Daily Star* (later changed to the *Star*), featuring colour pictures of half-naked women. Ingrams has never understood how a business-man could consider himself respectable if he published such material. Of course, Matthews might well have argued that the material in *Private Eye* was far more likely to give offence than his 'Gorgeous, pouting Starbirds in full living colour'.

In time, *Private Eye*'s attacks on Matthews began to alarm Junor because the Trafalgar boss was taking them to heart, so he fixed up a luncheon between Matthews and Ingrams, casting himself in the role of peacemaker. As a social event, this must have been something of a nightmare. Ingrams is a taciturn man, and Matthews is monosyllabic when not dis-cussing business. Junor sought to bridge the Grand Canyon between the tiny, brylcreemed tycoon and the large, corduroy-clad Oxford classical scholar by saying they all had one thing in common – a great love of newspapering. Both Ingrams and Matthews looked doubtful, but Jonah warmed to this theme.

'Don't you feel the hum of excitement just walking down Fleet Street, Victor, with the presses about to roar and the latest news flooding in from all over the world? Isn't it the most exciting place on earth?'

There was a long pause, reported Ingrams later. Then Matthews, in his flat, slightly polished Cockney tones, re-plied: 'No.'

Years later, Ingrams would rock with laughter as he dined out on the story. But he was on Junor's side, and thought it absurd that a man like 'Jonah' had to spend his life humouring boring businessmen like Victor Matthews. The stories about Matthews went on. One 'Grovel' item, unwittingly supplied by *Daily Mirror* editor Mike Molloy, concerned Matthews' false teeth. Molloy visited the dentist frequently because he ground his teeth in his sleep – 'Wouldn't you,' remarked a colleague, 'if you had seen the first edition of the *Mirror*?' On one occasion his dentist remarked that Matthews was one of his clients. Molloy expressed surprise that he had never seen Matthews in the waiting room. The dentist told him that Matthews did not visit – he sent the teeth round. They had to be cleaned often because he was very fond of whelks and other East End stall food.

From then on, Matthews became 'Lord Whelks' in *Private Eye*; and his son Ian became 'The Honourable Winkle'. When Lord Whelks, a noted 'I'm Backing Britain' patriot, sent one of his ships to be repaired in Malta rather than at a British yard, his nickname was extended to 'Lord Whelks of Valetta'. The 'Sir Jonah Junor' column in the *Eye* regularly called on Mrs Thatcher to further ennoble Lord Whelks, suggesting that a hereditary peerage might be in order for Britain's 'bonniest patriot'.

When Matthews, with Junor's help, got his life peerage, the front cover of the next issue of the *Eye* had a photograph of his head grafted onto a woman's naked body in a page-three pose. The caption read: 'STARLORD – Talk about a Burke's Peerage'. Ingrams was later told that Matthews had been so upset he had taken the day off.

Ingrams employed Junor's daughter Penny at *Private Eye*, which started her on the road to fame as Channel 4's consumer watchdog. He had liked a series Penny had written for the *Evening Standard*'s (as it then was) 'Londoner's Diary', testing the services of London hotels. All this entailed was booking into an expensive hotel and asking for some moderately difficult service, but it was well done. Her column was an oddity in *Private Eye* because it was 'straight', and it incensed Auberon Waugh in particular. He could never see the point in trying to seek redress on behalf of people foolish enough to have been taken advantage of by salesman. It brought to the *Eye* what he despised most – whingeing readers who wanted to use the magazine to save them from the consequences of what he regarded as their own stupidity.

Ingrams defended Penny's column, pointing to the huge stack of letters it received. This was not a very important point since he knew well that if you solicit letters, and offer such a watchdog service for nothing, it is hardly surprising if there is an abundant response. He was disappointed when Penny Junor decided to leave *Private Eye* for Channel 4. I was convinced that he had given Penny the job in part because she was Junor's daughter.

Penny's relationship with her father fascinates Ingrams, and he was intrigued by their appearance in a colour magazine feature called 'Relative Values', which he saved for his vast collection of clippings. He had appeared with Fred in the same feature and been very pleased with the result. Junor's comments about Penny in the article were all that you would expect of an adoring father, and more, while Penny's observations about 'Sir Jonah' were cool to the point of controversy. Ingrams wondered why Penny sounded so cool, and said: 'It's a terrible slap in the face for Sir Jonah.'

Junor is technically right-wing, but in fact his politics are those of the reigning Tory Prime Minister. Ingrams regards him as not dissimilar to Hudson, the Scottish butler played by Gordon Jackson in *Upstairs, Downstairs*. Whatever changes took place at the great house, Junor remained firmly in place. The new master had to be respected. Ingrams remembers Junor saying of Matthews: 'That little man could be another Beaverbrook.'

Private Eye has been supported by people on the far left and the far right – from Labour MP Brian Sedgemore to Alan Clark, wealthy heir to Lord Clark (of 'Civilization' fame). Sedgemore contributed interesting stories about barristers, and Clark was a star, if infrequent, guest at *Private Eye* lunches. Gnome House has also won the (qualified) approval of the centre, in the shape of David Steel, who says:

> Even though I have on occasions been totally traduced or misrepresented, I don't think I can say I have ever been hurt. Indeed, I think on one occasion when I wrote a letter correcting something it was duly published. But I do know of other people who have been hurt by it.

Perhaps *Private Eye*'s most unlikely fan has come recently in the shape of Marcia Williams, now Lady Falkender. In 1985 she lifted an *Eye* item about Robert Maxwell for her *Mail on Sunday* column. Since it became the subject of legal proceedings, I will confine myself to the account offered by Maxwell's own paper, the *Daily Mirror*. A prominent article in what was then the *Mirror* diary, headed 'ANOTHER WHOPPER!' ran:

> *Private Eye*, or Public Lie as it ought to be called, last week alleged that *Mirror* publisher Robert Maxwell was paying for Neil Kinnock's trip to Africa this week and that he had financed Kinnock's visit to Moscow last year.
>
> Not so.
>
> But that didn't stop Lady Marcia Falkender picking the story up and repeating it in her *Mail on Sunday* column yesterday.
>
> That is astonishing for two reasons:
>
> 1. When Marcia was Harold Wilson's secretary at Number Ten there was no newspaper or magazine she hated more than *Private Eye*. She said it always told lies about her.
>
> 2. Harold Wilson's office was largely financed by a number of private individuals and no one knew more about that than Lady Falkender.
>
> 3. Mr Maxwell last night wrote to the editor of the *Mail on Sunday*, Mr Stewart Steven, demanding a withdrawal of the allegation, an apology and a contribution of £25,000 to the *Mirror*'s appeal for the victims of the Ethiopean famine.
>
> Failing that, writs will be winging their way towards Mr

Steven and Lady Falkender – as well as *Private Eye*.

Mr Steven is, of course, well remembered for two 'whoppers'. First – while on the *Daily Express* – he discovered Martin Bormann, Hitler's deputy, living in South America. Needless to say, it wasn't Bormann. Then – while on the *Daily Mail* – he wrote a story about a Leyland slush fund. Another whopper – based on a forgery – which cost his proprietor several hundred thousand pounds in libel damages and legal costs.

Incidentally, Lady Falkender claims credit in her column for inventing the 'walkabout' by politicians. When she did it for Harold Wilson, she said, it 'contributed significantly to restoring his flagging fortunes'.

She omitted to point out that she invented the walkabout for the 1970 General Election.

Wilson lost.

Private Eye's friends and enemies are a diverse lot, and it is difficult to generalise about either group. Anyone who has been mercilessly teased or had their most embarrassing business or political secrets exposed in the magazine's pages is unlikely to feel well disposed towards Lord Gnome and his team of unruly wags. But broadly it appears to me that people who are content with the esteem in which they are held by those close to them have not taken attacks upon themselves as seriously as, say, journalists, businessmen and academics – especially those anxious to elevate themselves and their opinions. Politicians have generally proved themselves more than able to weather whatever storms *Private Eye* has brewed up around them. This is partly because no politician is going to reach a position of power without a skin at least as thick as a rhino's, partly because *Private Eye* has never taken a party political line, and partly because of the dangers inherent in any public confrontation over an item that the public at large may regard as no more than a joke.

But undoubtedly *Private Eye's* greatest friends are its readers, the vast majority of whom do not feature in its pages and probably never will. For them, *Private Eye's* real value probably lies in its persistent exposure and deflation of self-importance, hypocrisy, greed and corruption in public life.

Chapter Six

Whither the *Eye*?

In the early days, when Ian Hislop was still in nappies, Malcolm Muggeridge said *Private Eye* would soon become part of the Establishment, and was rewarded for his observation with the title Lord Buggeridge of Snide. Two decades later, Muggeridge's remark has become commonplace. In fact, it has never really been true. Had Ingrams been a social animal, it might have become so, for there were plenty of people who would have put him up for London clubs, but he says such places were for 'bores'.

What is true is that *Private Eye* has gained a wider acceptance among all kinds of people, crossing all age and social groupings. Cartoonist Michael Heath said he saw a group of young hooligans fighting over a copy, one saying: 'Gimme back me comic!' A book about the London police in 1986 recorded that members of a Special Patrol Group amused themselves by reading *Private Eye*.

Private Eye has long ceased to be a private joke or a country house party putting on a show for the servants, and it has moved into the mainstream of magazine publishing. Ingrams was invited to the annual luncheon of magazine editors, and in issue 642 (25 July 1986) a letter arrived offering 'market research activity' from a firm called The Research Marketing Consultancy Ltd. It was published, under the heading: 'Complete Bullshit'. Perhaps the letter was a joke, but it seems unlikely. For *Private Eye* is now mentioned regularly in the trade press.

The scurrilous reputation of *Private Eye* has always concealed its true nature, which is that of a small, flourishing, privately-owned business. Ingrams' decision to stay on as chairman and joke contributor has been seen as that of a tired satirist who just wants to stay around and make sure the new boys get it right. In fact, Ingrams, with some 400 shares, is the effective owner of a business which, if libel costs can be reduced, is capable of producing profits of around £250,000 a year.

A decision has been taken to reduce libel costs by exercising more care in the type of stories printed. Hislop explained to me that this entailed him reading the material more closely, and removing the lines most likely to attract a writ. He said that, with the best will in the world, Ingrams has not been able to do this in the latter days because he has been too tired. Perhaps so.

In July 1986 Ingrams let through a story about Donald Trelford, suggesting that the *Observer* editor was making use of an apartment in Covent Garden when he should have been at his office. This resulted in a letter from Trelford, dated 14 July, and later published in *Private Eye*:

Dear Richard,

You asked me last night if I was going to sue. This letter is written in the hope of avoiding that necessity. As you know, I have never complained or resorted to lawyers over the past decade, despite the many provocative and hurtful lies written about me in *Private Eye*.

But this week's story goes far beyond personal gossip. You say that I have grossly neglected my editorial duties at the most vital point in the week to pursue an affair at a specific date in a specific place. This is a malicious lie, but it is stated in such precise terms that people are likely to believe it. It has caused great distress to my wife and family and damage to by professional reputation. The facts are that between 3 and 6 pm last Saturday I was in India with my wife, taking part in a widely reported public debate in a stadium in Calcutta. We were also in India the previous Saturday. When I am in London I never leave the office at all on a Saturday, even for lunch, until the first, and usually the second, edition has gone to press. The story is a complete fabrication, as anyone at the *Observer* can testify.

I enclose the text of a correction I want published on the same page as the offending article in your next issue. If you refuse, or make no response by the end of Tuesday 15 July, I shall immediately hand the matter over to lawyers. That will mean going all the way with no holds barred – and you know me well enough to know I mean exactly what I say.

I hope to hear from you.

Yours Sincerely,
  Donald Trelford

Prior to the *Eye* item, the *Observer*'s diarist Peter Hillmore (Peter Pissmore in *Eye*-ese) had written a story suggesting Ingrams was drunk at a *Spectator* party. So Ingrams wrote back to Trelford:

Dear Donald,

As you know I have never complained or resorted to lawyers over the past few years, despite the many provocative and hurtful lies written about me in the *Observer*, and in particular by Peter Hillmore. But this week's story suggesting that I was drunk at the *Spectator* party and had to be restrained by my children from physically assaulting Mr Hillmore goes far beyond the bounds of fair comment. It has caused great distress to my wife who was not at the party and to my family.

The facts are that I arrived at the *Spectator* party at 8.45 pm, and did not have a single drink of any kind whatsoever. It will interest you to know that I have not partaken of alcoholic drink since 1967, so you will imagine the distress that has been caused by Mr Hillmore's last outrageous attack. I enclose the text of the correction I wish to be published on the same page as the offending article in the next issue of the *Observer*. If you refuse or make no response by the end of Tuesday 15 July, I shall immediately hand the matter over to lawyers. You should know me well enough to know that I mean exactly what I say.

I hope to hear from you.

Yours Sincerely,
  Richard Ingrams
  Editor

The *Observer* did carry a correction and an apology to Ingrams in Hillmore's next diary. But *Private Eye* chose to publish Trelford's letter, rather than his suggested correction. Ingrams also let it be known, to *Star* columnist Peter Tory, that the *Eye*'s euphemism for extra-marital sex, would henceforth be 'doing a Trelford'. Trelford issued a writ.

How might Hislop, had he been editor at the time, have prevented this action? He could have asked the author of the story if she was sure of her facts. She would have been unlikely to have said otherwise. He might have suggested that she make absolutely sure, by, say, ringing Trelford and asking him if the story was true. She would not have done so, for that would have exposed her as the would-be author.

In theory, Ingrams believes in reducing libel risk; in practice, less so. Hislop's decision, I believe, would have been to kill the item. And since there is virtually no way of proving what the *Eye* calls 'legover' stories, beyond getting those involved to admit them, the *Eye* once Ingrams vacates the editor's chair is likely, among other things, to be less ruthless in its pursuit of those engaged in 'Ugandan affairs'.

Nora Beloff once wrote that the *Eye* would be 'a slimmer and better' magazine if it took care to check its stories. But there is little evidence to suggest that people buy *Private Eye* because it tells the truth. It is far more likely that they buy it to smell a whiff of scandal. Even the saintly Lord Longford has admitted to the sinful enjoyment of reading the *Eye* in its old, untruthful form.

Ian Hislop told me he wanted to find 'new targets', drawn from personalities closer to his age group. It is hard to quarrel with this ambition, except to say that the *Eye* never became a success because of *who* it attacked so much as *how* it attacked them, be they Harold Macmillan or Boy George.

When Ingrams was Hislop's age he had already begun his long retreat into rural isolation and the sanctuary of cosy middle age, from which he savaged anything that was new and pushy. He lashed into contemporaries who went into the Foreign Office, the BBC, journalism and the City,

finding little to admire in modern life and much to con-
demn.

By contrast, Ian Hislop is part of the London scene. He
has worked for the BBC and for independent TV. His work
on *Spitting Image* seems likely to take more of his time in
future – a special show written for the Americans was
networked in the US by NBC in the autumn of 1986. Hislop
sees *Private Eye* in pragmatic terms. It is a going concern, its
joke products are popular, and his position as editor puts
him at the centre of Britain's satire industry.

Hislop resents admen, various entertainment personalities, Mrs Thatcher and Fleet Street journalists. But he
is not a big-time hater in the Ingrams league. It is incon-
ceivable that he would ever risk going to prison over a story.
Neither is he ever likely to risk bankrupting *Private Eye* over
a feud.

Unlike Ingrams, he is not a moral crusader. He will print
'legover' stories for amusement, if they are safe legally;
Ingrams printed them because he disapproved of adultery.
Hislop says he will check all stories carefully for libel;
Ingrams compared *Eye* items to the Holy Gospels. He said
in 1986, during an interview with the Roman Catholic
weekly, the *Universe*:

> I'm always struck by the resemblance of the Gospels with
> stories that get into the *Eye*. That sounds a very blasphemous
> thing to say. But they [the Gospels] are full of inaccuracies that
> don't add up and things that are obviously wrong. People
> always say, 'Oh, that means that they can't be true.' My
> assumption as a journalist is that they are true because of that.
>
> Graham Greene said the same. When he reads the Gospels
> he knows it's true because of certain little details in it – like a
> man racing the other disciple to the Tomb.

Ingrams sees *Private Eye* as a moral force, and the image of
him which has generally been accepted in 1986 is of a tired
crusader handing his sword to a younger man. The reality is
different. Ingrams will continue to run *Private Eye*, working
three days a fortnight. He has taken on a fortnightly

column, at £450 a piece, in the *Sunday Telegraph*. He will continue to take part in radio and TV programmes, and has several book projects in the offing.

His calculation is that *Private Eye*, edited by Ian Hislop, will continue to make money – indeed, it will probably make more money if libel actions are avoided. He is the effective owner of a magazine he seized control of twenty-three years ago, which might now be worth, on the basis of its profitability, more than a million pounds.

Ingrams now personally owns property worth perhaps £300,000, and his earnings cannot be less than £50,000. Even if Hislop is an outright failure as editor, *Private Eye* is likely to coast for at least ten years on the momentum it has built up.

Ingrams told me late in July 1986 that he was staying on at *Private Eye* because, 'I need the money.' What does he need it for? His two children are grown up, and he leads a very simple life. Moreover, his earnings from outside the *Eye* – from newspapers, magazines, broadcasting and books – could, without very great effort on his part, exceed £40,000 a year.

My conviction is that Ingrams sees the *Eye* as a good business which he has built and that he likes the idea of it being there to provide him with a comfortable middle age and retirement. And what could possibly be wrong with that?

In our conversations about the nature of *Private Eye* I have often said to Ingrams that I see the *Eye* as a magazine which, by its very nature, must always be on the brink of bankruptcy. If it is not, there seems little ethical justification for it surviving at all – and at the very least its crusading image must suffer if it appears to be highly profitable.

Private Eye under Ingrams has built up a huge readership because it has taken chances – for which it has often been punished in the courts. But there is no question that *Private Eye*'s losses in the courts and its highly-publicised public rows have added to its allure. People by and large do not read *Private Eye* because they see it as a last repository of truth; they read it because it strays over the border of what is permissible and tasteful in its attempts to peer beneath the public face of the rich and famous.

Ingrams replies that it was fine for the *Eye* to have a poor bank balance in the early days, when libel costs were lower; but now that prospective litigants know the *Eye* makes money, they sue more frequently, and legal costs are higher. The *Eye* needs to be wealthy if it is to go on living dangerously. This sounds plausible enough, but it is not the whole truth. In the sixties and the seventies, *Private Eye* was threatened with closure on a number of occasions because of libel actions. In the eighties that has not been the case, not even in a year in which one action alone cost over £200,000.

The immediate effect of huge libel bills in the 1980s was not to threaten the future of the paper so much as the earnings of those who worked for it. *Private Eye*, as I have mentioned earlier, distributes its profits among its contributors in the form of bonuses. Their fortnightly cheques are doubled until the profit is consumed. But money is also put aside for a rainy day, and invested in the paper's infrastructure. For instance, the *Eye* owns outright a longish lease at number 6 Carlisle Street, an area of Soho which is much sought after, in addition to the property in south London where the subscription and distribution staff work.

Ingrams has little to lose if Hislop makes the *Eye* safer. Indeed, in the short term, he might very well have much to gain. The magazine may become bland, but it could take readers years to notice this, especially if the joke pages maintain a rude, irreverent (and legally safe) zing to them. And if the *Eye* does change noticeably for the worse, Ingrams will be seen as the man who, in his day, made it great.

Ian Hislop plans to extend the *Eye*'s joke material into records and, perhaps, video tapes. There is even a possibility of the *Eye* moving into television comedy. However, there are no plans to increase, or harden, the *Eye*'s news pages. Dave Cash believes this should be done by, in his own words, 'hiring a professional hack' to run the non-joke pages. But Hislop, supported by Ingrams, has resisted the idea.

To many of us, Paul Foot would have been the perfect choice as Ingrams' successor. He works for Robert Maxwell's *Daily Mirror*, and earns perhaps £20,000 there. But Foot has never been in journalism for money, and in any case the *Eye* could easily afford to match Maxwell's terms – indeed, Ingrams, Cash and Tony Rushton all make more money than Foot for far less arduous work.

No one has ever written the back pages as well as Foot, who combined passion with considerable precision. Ingrams says that Ian Hislop is a good hater – 'he really hates Thatcher, Jeffrey Archer and people like that' – but he is not in Foot's league. Hislop, it appears to me, hates politicians for much the same superficial reason that he hates admen – for their mannerisms and attitudes.

There is no reason to suppose that Foot would have joined the *Eye* again for a third time, even if he had been invited to do so. But it is certain that, had he done so, Ingrams would not be able to anticipate a restful retirement.

What seems to me to have happened is this: the *Eye* has built up a mighty readership with highly-publicised libel cases and a penchant for going further than Fleet Street. Readers attracted by the clamorous publicity have found much else to enjoy in its pages, and Ingrams has been able to use this as a basis for launching and maintaining excellent jokes such as 'Dear Bill', and the host of other *Eye* book spin-offs. With the assistance of W. H. Smith and Menzies, the *Eye* has reached a new sales plateau of nearly a quarter of a million a fortnight. For Ingrams, it was an opportune moment to ease off.

Here, another dimension of his character is worth studying. Old friends such as Auberon Waugh have found Ingrams increasingly censorious and disapproving. In 1986 he is moving closer to the Roman Catholic Church. In an interview about his beliefs, he said:

I think it's very possible I might become a Catholic one day. I took instruction from Father Michael Hollings when I was at Oxford, but I never persevered with it and it fizzled out when I left. Partly why Malcolm Muggeridge became a Catholic in the end was that he'd always had an aversion to abortion and birth control. I don't feel nearly as strongly as that. On the other hand, I do agree with the church about divorce. The idea of people getting re-married in church – which the Church of England toys with – I find very distasteful.

I was brought up in a funny family situation, one of four brothers. My mother was – and still is – a Catholic, my father was a Protestant. They reached a peculiar compromise. They divided us up – two Catholics, two Protestants. I was in the Protestant half. It worked out alternately. My elder brother was a Catholic, I was a Protestant, the next brother Catholic, the younger brother Protestant.

It was rather like being in Northern Ireland in a way. There were definitely two religious camps. My father was away a lot, so I was very much under the influence of my mother, who is a devout Catholic. She turned me on to religion, taught me how to say my prayers. I pray regularly, sometimes on the train. I find myself more inclined to think about religious matters in Soho rather than in the country. People think if you live in the country you see the birds and the trees and your thoughts turn to God. I don't find that much. I'm more inclined to think about such things wandering about Soho among the strip clubs. It makes you think about the nature of people.

My wife is a Catholic. So are my children. What starts you re-thinking about religion is when you have children. You begin to worry about what they are going to believe in. The children won't practise their religion, but I feel they will prob-ably come back. Both of them are basically religious people. And I don't have any misgivings on that score.

My wife is a Catholic convert, and I think my mother had a considerable hand in that. It's extraordinary how my mother converts people to Catholicism. All her daughters-in-law have become Catholics. We were severely put to the test having a mentally-handicapped child, Arthur. He wasn't able to do anything at all and it put a great strain on everyone. People who don't have experience of that sort of thing don't really realise. They see everything ticking over and they don't really know. I was helped by having some religious faith at this time. Am I confident Arthur is in Heaven now? Yes.

People sometimes ask me how I equate my *Private Eye* work with my faith, and accuse one of hypocrisy. All I can say is that I don't experience any personal doubts, any conscience about it. But that probably sounds smug on my part. I always think journalists are better able to believe in Christianity than, say, clergymen.

What am I most grateful for? My family and my love of music, the great composers like Bach. I sit in concerts with tears running down my face. I go to the *St Matthew Passion* every year and I always feel that it's not going to move me. But it always does.

Another thing I'm very grateful for is that I have always been able to do things that I have enjoyed. The majority of people do jobs they dislike and it gets them down. I've always been in the very fortunate position of doing something I enjoy and being my own boss, which is a terrific advantage in life.

My greatest shortcomings are intolerance, sloth and slap-dashery. I find it very difficult to concentrate on anything. I am very easily bored. I don't think I have been easy to live with. My only advantage is that I am undemanding about things like food. I don't expect grand meals. But I do sit in silence most of the time and I am anti-social. I hope to improve on this. Ever-lasting life is not an idea that particularly appeals to me. There are quite a lot of people I would not want to meet in heaven – Esther Rantzen, Jeffrey Archer, Arthur Scargill. There are so many . . .

If Ingrams sounds like Muggeridge, who is almost forty years his senior, perhaps it is not surprising. He is Muggeridge's official biographer, and has spent much time with the old journalist-seer in Robertsbridge, East Sussex. He also sounds like the Earl of Longford, who also paces the streets of Soho buried in the contemplation of sin and sinners.

Perhaps because his own father died when he was fifteen, Ingrams has always sought out old men. He reveres Graham Greene and Claud Cockburn, Lord Denning and Muggeridge. His first full-length book, *God's Apology*, was a sensitive study of the lifelong friendship between three men. He championed the case of P. J. Wodehouse, and published a collection of the works of H. B. Morton, author for fifty years of the 'Beachcomber' satirical column. He was a friend of Douglas Bader, the wartime flying ace, and of the late pocket cartoonist Osbert Lancaster.

Ingrams was off work for two months in 1985 with back troubles, and it was during this period that Ian Hislop confirmed his position as the future editor. Ingrams was grateful to Hislop, and rightly so. He had never been away for so long before, and this time the *Eye* got along well enough without him. Mary Ingrams was naturally concerned about Richard's health, and I think his decision to retire from the editorship was made then. Muggeridge was among the first to congratulate him.

He has never said as much to me, but I feel that he fears he might not live to be an old man. For over twenty years he has put most of his energy into building up *Private Eye*, and I think he has calculated that it will carry him safely into full retirement. That would surely be less certain if *Private Eye*'s new editor were fired with anything like Ingrams' early zeal and moral anger.

GLOSSARY OF GNOMESPEAK

Leo Abscess: Leo Abse, Labour politician.

James 'Toady' Adams: James Adams, right-hand man of *Sunday Times* editor Andrew Neil.

George G. Ale: George Gale, broadcaster and journalist.

Tariq Tin Pan Ali: Tariq Ali, left-wing agitator.

Arkell v. Pressdram: This refers to a lawsuit brought by James Arkell, the Granada Group's retail credit manager, against *Private Eye*, which alleged that Arkell received a retainer each month from a debt agency after getting them the Granada contract. His lawyers, Goodman, Derrick & Co., sent the *Eye* a letter saying that Arkell's attitude to damages would be governed by the nature of its reply. The *Eye* replied, in print, that the nature of our reply is as follows: "fuck off".' The case was dropped.

Low Arse: A. L. Rowse, historian.

Asthma: The trade union ASTMS.

Baby Susan: Waugh's name for Zara Phillips, Princess Anne's daughter. Waugh reported that her parents had intended to call her Sarah but that their strange pronunciation was misunderstood and she 'got lumbered with a Jewish boy's name'.

The Badger: Ron Hall, *Sunday Times* journalist and badger lookalike who was involved in infiltrating *Eye* lunches.

Baldilocks: Gerald Kaufmann, Labour politician.

Nora Ballsoff: Miss Nora Beloff, then political correspondent of the *Observer*, who sued *Private Eye* for publishing a private memorandum she had sent to her editor suggesting she wrote a sympathetic piece about Maudling, whom the *Eye* was investigating. The 'Ballsoff Fund' was set up to help pay the court costs.

Melvyn Barg: Melvyn Bragg, TV arts presenter.

Tina Barg: Tina Brown, journalist and girlfriend of Harold Evans.

Bat Ears: Waugh on Prince Charles (qv *Brian*).

Evelyn Baugh: Evelyn Waugh, writer.

The Beast: Journalist Anthony Haden-Guest, some of whose social habits the *Eye* found unsavoury (qv *Anthony Uninvited-Guest*).

The Beast of South Street: Sir John Davis, Rank chief.

Sir Reginald Beaujolais: Reggie Bosanquet (qv *Reginald Boozanquet*).

Beaverkin: Jonathan Aitken, Beaverbrook's grandson, Tory politician.

Benito: Brian Hitchin, Mussolini lookalike and London editor of the *Daily Star*.

Ross 'Pretty Boy' Benson: Ross Benson, handsome *Express* journalist.

John 'Pretty Thing' Bentley: John Bentley, a good-looking financier.

Sir John Betjeperson: Sir John Betjeman.

Adrian Berri-Berri: The *Eye*'s science correspondent after Adrian Berry, the science correspondence of the *Daily Telegraph*.

Biggles: Sir Max Aitken, Lord Beaverbrook's son, a wartime flying ace.

Black Bob: Bob Geldof.

The Black Knight: Andrew Knight, *Telegraph* executive.

Bovver Booth: East End starlet Pat Booth.

Reginald Boozanquet: Reginald Bosanquet, tipsy TV newscaster.

Joan Borewell: Joan Bakewell, TV reporter.

The Boss: Margaret Thatcher in 'Dear Bill'.

Botney: Alan Yentob, BBC editor of *Arena*.

The Bouncing Czech: Robert Maxwell, Eastern European-born publisher (qv *Cap'n Bob*).

The Boy David: David Steel, boyish Liberal leader.

Brenda: the Queen – Dempster's name for her.

Brian: Prince Charles (qv *Bat Ears*).

Michael Brilliantine: Michael Heseltine, blond shaggy-locked Tory politician (qv *Tarzan* and *Gingernuts*).

Brillo Pad: Andrew Neil, *Sunday Times* editor.

Dracula Brittan: Leon Brittan, Tory politician, in 'Dear Bill'.

Saturday Night Fever Brown: Louis Brown, owner of the Valbonne nightclub and Skindles Hotel, Maidenhead.

Alistair Brunette: Alistair Burnett, TV newscaster.

Basil Brush: *Daily Express* editor (1974) Ian McColl, a small Scotsman with a piping voice (qv *Ian 'Chips and 4 Forks' McColl*).

Bubbles: Viscountess Rothermere, formerly dancer Beverly Brooks, a Rank Charm School graduate of the early 1950s. The name was coined by Dempster, who noted her love of champagne.

Lord Buggeridge of Snide: Malcolm Muggeridge, who had suggested that the *Eye* satirists used 'a bazooka rather than poisoned arrows', and that with their 'largely Top People' clientele, would soon be accepted by the Establishment.

Andy Bumhol: Andy Warhol, androgynous pop artist.

Bunter: Nicholas Soames, son of 'Fatty', Lord Soames.

The Cad: Peter Cadbury, much-married businessman.

Cap'n Bob: Robert Maxwell, because of his battlefield commission in the war (qv *The Bouncing Czech*).

Sir Huge Carlton-Towers: Sir Hugh Carleton-Greene, the lofty ex-BBC Director-General.

Peter Carter-Fuck: Peter Carter-Ruck, libel lawyer who represents many of the *Eye*'s plaintiffs.

Chateau Despair: the *Daily Express* (qv *The Lubianka*).

Cheryl: Princess Diana's (*Eye*'s name) (qv *Brenda*, *Brian*, *Yvonne*).

The Chingford Skinhead: Norman Tebbit, balding Tory

politician (Chingford) with a reputation for putting the boot in (qv *Mr Munster*).

Lord Clark of Civilisation: Lord Clark, whose book on culture through the ages, *Civilisation*, was a bestseller.

Mr Clean: Victor Lownes (qv *Disgusting*).

Dr Donald Cobweb: Dr Donald Coggan, Archbishop of Canterbury.

Cock of the North/Beast of Bouverie Street/I Ask You: All referred to Barry Askew, ex-editor of the *News of the World* and a noted northern philanderer.

Colour Section: Started at the front of the magazine when the *Observer* launched its colour magazine. *Private Eye*'s remained firmly black and white.

The Corsican Brothers: Saatchi & Saatchi, Tory advertising agents, in 'Dear Bill'.

Aidan 'Creepy' Crawley: LWT's executive director (1971).

Alistair Creak: Alistair Cooke, broadcaster and journalist.

Richard Crossbum: Richard Crossman, Labour politician and diarist.

Cyclops: Dermot Purgavie, former *Now!* journalist with one eye, also a *Mail* correspondent in New York.

Daily Getsworse (later, *Daily Getsmuchworse*): *Daily Express*.

Daily Smut: *Daily Star*, launched in 1978.

Daily Tits-by-Christmas: the *Daily Express*, after its take-over by Lord Matthews.

Daisy: Richard Compton Miller, gossip columnist. The name was coined by rival diarist Adrian Woodhouse.

Unter/Oonter Davies: Hunter Davies, northern journalist and author.

Herr Wilhelm 'Rudi' Davis: William Davis, *Punch* editor, who had German antecedents (qv *Kaiser Bill*).

Sean Day-Telegraph: Sean Day-Lewis, *Daily Telegraph* TV writer.

Sneakin Deakin: Michael Deakin, unpopular TV-am executive.

Dr Death: Dr David Owen, SDP leader (qv *Dr Kildare*).

Dezzie: Desmond Wilcox, TV presenter and journalist.

Digger: Richard Neville, the Australian editor of the underground magazine *Oz*.

David Dimblebore: David Dimbleby, son of Richard.

Richard Dimblebore/Bumbleby: Broadcaster Richard Dimbleby.

Dirty Dai: Dai Llewellyn, son of Colonel Harry Llewellyn.

The Dirty Digger: Australian publisher Rupert Murdoch.

Disgusting: Victor Lownes, *Playboy* publisher whose jacuzzi parties at his country house, Stocks, were notorious for hanky panky (qv *Mr Clean*).

Alastair Ditherington: Alastair Hetherington, ex-*Guardian* editor.

Doing a Guinness: Urinating – based on a Grovel report that Camilla and Penny Guinness had relieved themselves into a gondola in Venice.

Margaret Drivel: Margaret Drabble, author.

The Dusky Handmaiden: Maiko Lee, a hand model and escort of Viscount Rothermere.

Dame Harold Evans: Harold Evans, former editor of the *Sunday Times*, who was nicknamed Dame Harold Evans (after Dame Edith Evans) by Lord Arran, who thought him pompous, in his *Evening News* column. Hence also the *Sunday Dames* for the *Sunday Times*.

Lord Excrement: Lord Egremont, Macmillan's private secretary.

Marijuana Faithful: Marianne Faithful, singer and Jagger girlfriend.

Lord and Lady Fartwell: Lord and Lady Hartwell, proprietors of the *Daily Telegraph*.

The Fat Man/Fats: Alex Herbage, vast, dodgy financier.

Fattersly: Roy Hattersly, Labour politician, in 'Dear Bill' (qv *Hatterji*).

Sir David Fester: Sir David English, *Daily Mail* editor, who described a story about the *Mail* in the *Eye* as a 'festering lie'.

Fingers: Lord Matthews, proprietor of Express Newspapers,

so called because Nigel Dempster claimed he had abnormally large fingers (qv *Lord Whelks*).

Mr Fixit: Adnan Khashoggi, Saudi billionaire arms dealer.

The Flame-Haired Temptress: Audrey Slaughter, journalist and second wife of Charles Wintour.

Fog: Mark Phillips. The *Eye* reported that this was his Sandhurst nickname because he was 'thick and wet'.

Captain Foulenough: John Elliot, *Tatler* publisher (1979), after a 'Beachcomber' character.

Foxhunter: Colonel Harry Llewellyn, father of Dai and Roddy and owner of the Olympic prize-winning horse, Foxhunter.

The Fragrant Doyenne: Lady Olga Maitland, *Sunday Express* gossip columnist.

Lady Magnesia Freelove: Lady Antonia Fraser who, according to the *Eye*, told a lovesick Clive James, 'I only sleep with the First XI.'

Frigid Frophy: Brigid Brophy, author.

David Frosd: David Frost, TV personality with adenoidal trouble (qv *Gipsy Dave*).

Miss Gay Funloving: Appeared at the time of Christine Keeler, star of the Profumo scandal.

Lord Gannex: Lord Kagan, manufacturer of Gannex coats favoured by Harold Wilson, who ennobled him.

Bamber Gasket: Bamber Gascoigne, TV host.

Get on with it! This exhortation was probably first used by Richard Berens, then William Hickey, whose practice it was to return unsteadily from Boodles at four in the afternoon and bellow through the door to spur on the toiling hacks in his employ. The choleric George Gale used it later to great effect on the hapless folk who rang up his radio phone-in programme to express their views on current affairs.

Gingernuts: Michael Heseltine (qv *Michael Brilliantine* and *Tarzan*).

Gipsy Dave: TV personality David Frost (qv *David Frosd*).

Sunken Glandys: Duncan Sandys, Tory politician.

Lord Gnome: Richard Ingrams, editor of the *Eye* since 1962. The character of Lord Gnome is loosely based on Lord Beaverbrook.

'Goldenballs': The fund the *Eye* set up for readers' donations to help fight the Goldsmith action.

Sir James Goldfinger/Sir Jams/Sir Jammy Fishpaste etc: All variations on Sir James Goldsmith, the millionaire food tycoon and *Private Eye*'s greatest enemy, who in January 1976 issued over sixty libel writs against the magazine and thirty-seven of its distributors. At the same time he applied to the High Court to bring an action for criminal libel against the *Eye*.

The Blessed Arnold Goodman: The lawyer Lord Goodman, the first subject of the *Eye*'s series 'The Lives of the Saints' (qv *Two Dinners*).

Lord Goodmanzee: Lord Goodman, likened to a chimpanzee (qv *Two Dinners* and *The Blessed Arnold Goodman*).

Gorbals: Charlie Wilson, *Times* executive with Glaswegian temperament and language to match – also known as *McNasty* and *Charlie Foulmouth*.

Gorgeous George: George Howard, the late BBC chairman.

Joe Gormless: Joe Gormley, ex-miners' leader.

The Grauniad: the *Guardian*, so called because of its frequent typesetting errors.

Sir Sidney Gravytrain: Sir Sidney Bernstein, ex-Granada TV boss.

Grease: Gordon Reece, Thatcher's image-making PR man.

Greatest Living Englishman: Nigel Dempster, as described by Auberon Waugh (qv *Humpty Dumpster* and *Pratt-Dumpster*).

Low Greed/Low Grade: Lord Lew Grade, entertainments empire boss.

The Greek Pudding: Arianna Stassinopoulos, Greek-born writer and socialite.

Grovel: the *Eye*'s gossip column, started by Patrick Marnham. The name came from the old Charles Greville column in the *Daily Mail*.

Anthony Uninvited-Guest: Anthony Haden-Guest, louche journalist and gatecrasher (qv *The Beast*).

Worzel Gummidge: Michael Foot, leader of the Labour Party.

Sir William Haley Mills: Sir William Haley, former *Times* editor.

Halitosis Hall: the House of Commons in 'Dear Bill'.

Allan 'Plug 'Em All' Hall: Allan Hall, 'Atticus' editor of the *Sunday Times* (1974) and freebie expert.

Mere Harmsworth: Vere Harmsworth, who became Viscount Rothermere.

Kenneth Harris Tweed: Kenneth Harris, long-standing *Observer* journalist.

Roy Hatterji: Roy Hattersley, Labour politician, who has many Asians in his constituency, the Sparkbrook division of Birmingham.

Union Jack Hayward: Jack Hayward, super-patriot, donator to the Liberal Party and tax exile.

Bomber Healey: Denis Healey, Labour politician.

Grocer Heath: Ted Heath, so called because of his 1962 Common Market negotiations.

Hissing Sid: Charles Wintour, ex-*Evening Standard* editor, whom the *Eye* throught resembled the comic strip snake of the same name (qv *Sir Charles Mostyn-Wintour*).

Christopher 'Robin' Hitchens: boyish, left-wing scribe.

Hitler: Max Hastings, journalist and war correspondent, now editor of the *Daily Telegraph*.

Homosexualist: Word coined by Auberon Waugh to compete with feminist, sexist, etc.

Hopalong: President Reagan in 'Dear Bill'.

Dominic Horrid (our economic staff): Dominic Harrod, BBC economics editor.

Anthony Wedgwood Hoverbene: Anthony Wedgwood Benn, Labour politician.

George Hoverbrown/Lloyd George Brown: George Brown, Labour politician.

The Human Gorilla: John Aspinall, private zoo and casino owner.

Humpty-Dumpster: Nigel Dempster, so called after his enforced departure from the *Eye* after he had denied in an interview with the *Sunday Times* that he had anything to do with a Grovel item on Cecil Parkinson, over which Parkinson was suing. The *Eye* thought differently (qv *Greatest Living Englishman* and *Pratt-Dumpster*).

Virginia Ironbackside: Virginia Ironside, columnist.
Clive 'Mussolini' Irving: *Times* journalist hoaxed into believing he had found Mussolini's diaries.

The Jackal: Paul Callan, *Mirror* journalist.
Clive Jaws: Clive James, critic (qv *Magwitch*).
Sir Peter Jaybotham: Sir Peter Jay, Ambassador to USA who succeeded Sir Peter Ramsbotham.
Peter Jay-Cloth: Peter Jay, TV presenter and economist.
Fat Cat Jenkins: Roy Jenkins in 'Dear Bill' (qv *Smoothiechops* and *Woy Jenkins*).
Woy Jenkins: Roy Jenkins, the SDP politician who cannot pronounce his r's (qv *Smoothiechops* and *Fat Cat Jenkins*).
Loony Bins Johnson: L.B.J., U.S. President, later used about journalist Paul Johnson.
Sir Sheath Joseph: Sir Keith Joseph, Tory politician (qv *The Mad Monk*).

Kaiser Bill: William Davis, *Punch* editor (qv *Herr Wilhelm 'Rudi' Davis*).
Kanga: Dale Tryon, Australian wife of Lord Tryon and a friend of Prince Charles.
Ludicrous Kennedy: Ludovic Kennedy, television personality.
Henry 'Scotch Eggs' Keswick: Henry Keswick, ex-proprietor of the *Spectator*, who had a weakness for scotch eggs.
Dr Kildare: Dr David Owen, SDP leader (qv *Dr Death*).
Hans Killer: Hans Keller, music critic.
Kinnochio: Neil Kinnock, Labour leader.
Hairy Knees: Airey Neave, Tory politician.

Freddy 'Fly by Night' Laker: Freddie Laker of the defunct

Laker Airways.

Sir Larold Lamb: Sir Larry Lamb (qv *Sir Tit and Bum*).

Leninspart/Red Ken: Ken Livingstone, left-wing former GLC leader.

Little Shit: Martin Amis, author and journalist, son of Kingsley, who set competitions in the *New Statesman* under the name 'Little Keith'.

Lord Liver of Cesspool: Lord Russell of Liverpool, who brought one of the *Eye's* first big libel cases.

Enoch Loonie-Powell: Enoch Powell, Tory politician of extreme views.

The Lubianka: The shiny black art deco *Daily Express* building, which the *Eye* likened to the legendary Russian prison and torture chamber (qv *Château Despair*).

Edward Lucie-Pseud: Edward Lucie-Smith, art critic.

Mabel Lucie-Smith: Edward Lucie-Smith, art critic.

Harold Maciavillain: Harold Macmillan.

The Mad Monk: Sir Keith Joseph, after Rasputin (qv *Sir Sheath Joseph*).

Captain Magic: *Express* editor Chistopher Ward.

Magwitch: Clive James (qv *Clive Jaws*).

The Marfia: The group of men in Marcia Falkender's circle.

The Marmite Train: *Now!* magazine owned by Sir James Goldsmith (*The Marmite King* – he also owned Marmite as part of his food empire). Huge salaries and expenses were being proffered to climb aboard, and the *Eye* contemptuously monitored those who accepted the *'Bovril shilling'*.

Richard 'Alfie' Marsh: Richard Marsh, after the wide-boy character in the film *Alfie*.

Antonio Di Masturbani: Antonioni, arty Italian film director.

Maverick: Mike Molloy, poker-playing editor of the *Daily Mirror*.

Rene McAlcoholl: Rene McColl, *Daily Express* foreign correspondent.

Ian 'Chips and 4 Forks' McColl: Ian McColl, editor of the *Daily Express* in 1972, known for his late night supper activities in the office (qv *Basil Brush*).

Lavish McTavish: Simon Courtauld, deputy editor of the *Spectator* (1979) with parsimonious habits; said to have been banned from a golf course for excessive hunting of tees.

Farty Meldman: Marty Feldman, comedian.

George 'Thoroughly Modern' Melly: George Melly, jazz musician and writer.

Mogadon Man: Geoffrey Howe, Tory politician, in 'Dear Bill'.

Miss Moneybags: the heiress Mrs Vivien Duffield, née Clore.

Hugh Montgomery-Massivesnob: Hugh Montgomery-Massingberd, genealogist.

Sir Charles Mostyn-Wintour: Charles Wintour, ex-*Evening Standard* editor, called 'Sir' because he had been denied a longed-for knighthood, and 'Mostyn' because the Italian lady journalist he was keen on at the time (Gaia Servadio) was married to Sir Willie Mostyn (qv *Hissing Sid*).

Mr Munster: Norman Tebbit, Tory politician, in 'Dear Bill' (qv *The Chingford Skinhead*).

Campbell Murdoch: John Wells' early pseudonym.

Lenin Murray: Len Murray, former TUC leader.

Sir Gerald 'Che' Nabarro/Sir Gerald Nohandlebarrow: Sir Gerald Nabarro, Tory politician.

Mr Nicely Nicely: Nigel Lawson, Tory politician, in 'Dear Bill'.

Geraldine Normal, our saleroom correspondent: based on Geraldine Norman, saleroom correspondent for *The Times*.

NOTSOBA: a rendering of the print union NATSOPA.

Conor Cruise O'Booze: Conor Cruise O'Brien, *Observer* commentator.

Edna O'Booze: Edna O'Brien, novelist.

Lunchtime O'Booze: the *Eye*'s fictitious reporter whose name changed according to his venue or story: when in Vietnam he became *Lun-Tai-O-Boos*; in Germany *Lunch-*

time O' Boche and in Greece, *Lunchtime Ob. Ouzo*. His famous line is: 'One thingsh shertain, nushin will ever be the same again.'

Old Catseyes: Enoch Powell, Tory politician, in 'Dear Bill'.

Kenneth Oldschooltynan: Kenneth Tynan, theatre critic.

The One-Armed Bandit: One-armed Tory politician William Rees-Davies.

John Osbore/Osbum: John Osborne, playwright.

Oyster Eyes: Willie Whitelaw, Tory politician.

Colonel Bruce Page: Bruce Page, *New Statesman* editor, who Patrick Marnham claimed was a KGB colonel.

Pass the sick bag, Alice!: an alleged Junor expression, and frequently used thereafter in the *Eye* spoof of his *Sunday Express* column.

Peterbore: The column Peterborough in the *Daily Telegraph*.

Prince Philistine: Prince Philip.

Miss Piggy: Emma Soames, journalist daughter of Lord Soames.

Piranha Teeth: Jocelyn Stevens, ex-*Daily Express* supremo with a notorious temper. The name was reportedly coined by the Earl of Lichfield.

Piss-poor: Alleged to have been first used by Sir John Junor, editor of the *Sunday Express*, to Lady Olga Maitland about her gossip column in the paper.

Peter Pisspoor: Peter Hillmore, *Observer* diarist.

Roy Plugmey: Roy Plumley, former host of *Desert Island Discs*.

The Poisoned Carrot: Nicholas Witchell, red-haired TV newscaster.

Poove/Pouftah: coined by Jeremy Geidt, member of the Establishment nightclub, to mean homosexual.

Lord Popeye: Lord Weidenfeld, the publisher. Grovel reported that his eyes popped out at moments of amatory excitement and had to be gently returned to their sockets with a warm silver spoon.

Lord Porn: Lord Longford, veteran campaigner against pornography.

Pratt-Dumpster: Dempster's nickname after his new entry in

Who's Who revealed his father's middle name to be 'Pratt' (qv *Greatest Living Englishman* and *Humpty-Dumpster*).

Pseud: a noun coined at Shrewsbury by Ingrams from pseudo-intellectual, meaning pretentious person.

Chapman Puncher/Bottom Pincher: Chapman Pincher, *Daily Express* defence writer.

Colonel Libby Purves: Libby Purves, hearty radio presenter.

Princess Pushy: the *Eye*'s own name for Princess Michael of Kent (qv *Our Val* and *Princess Tom*).

Sir Alec Quatervass: Sir Alec Douglas-Home (qv *Baillie Vass*).

Mary Quunt: Mary Quant.

Enid Rancid: Esther Rantzen (qv *Teeth*).

Rigid Man: journalist Geoffrey Wheatcroft, known by this appellation ever since Jeffrey Bernard described in the *Spectator* how he 'keeled over with a crate of tonics at Cheltenham races and came to rest in a horizontal position . . . rigor mortis set in although the patient was far from dead' (qv *Geoffrey Wheatgerm*).

Angela Ripping: Angela Rippon.

Royal Midget: Princess Margaret (qv *Yvonne*).

Killer Runcie: Robert Runcie, Archbishop of Canterbury, so called because of the number of Germans the *Eye* said he boasted of having killed in the war as a Scots Guard.

Runcieballs: Archbishop Runcie.

Sad: Gay, coined by Richard Ingrams.

Barry 'Off' Sales: Barry Sales, Thames TV executive.

Anatomy Sampson: Anthony Sampson, author of *Anatomy of Britain*.

Adolf Scargill: Arthur Scargill, NUM leader.

Milton Schoolmarm: Milton Schulman, *Evening Standard* theatre critic.

Dr Roger Scrotum: Dr Roger Scruton, Tory philosopher and author of a book on sex.

Peter Sellout: Peter Sellers, who took off to work in the USA.

The Sherpa/The Nepalese: Anthony Howard, *Observer*

journalist, because of his oriental features.

Shirl the Pearl: Shirley Williams, SDP politician.

The Shit of Persia: the Shah of Persia.

Shurely shome mishtake: A reference to William Deedes (Bill Deedesh), editor of the *Daily Telegraph*, who pronounces 's' as 'sh' – a speech impediment thought to have been adopted many years ago on the grounds that it made him sound even more distinguished.

Glenda Slag: Based on Jean Rook, columnist.

Lady Slagheap: Lady Falkender, because of her connection with the slagheap affair – one of the Wilson era scandals. She was also known as *Lady Forkbender*.

David Slick: David Hicks, interior designer.

'Slicker': Michael Gillard, who looks after the city pages.

Slimy: Bernard Shrimsley, Tony's brother and editor of the *News of the World*. Together Waugh referred to him and his brother (qv *Toady*) as the Brothers Shrim.

The Smellysocks Brigade: Union leaders, Labour supporters, etc. in 'Dear Bill'.

Smoothiechops: Roy Jenkins, when a Labour front bencher (qv *Woy Jenkins* and *Fat Cat Jenkins*).

W. H. Smugg/Smug/Smut: The national newsagents who refused to sell *Private Eye* until 1985, after Menzies accepted it.

C. P. Snurd: C. P. Snow, author.

Fatty Soames: Lord Soames, a large figure in the Tory Party.

Stewart 'Bormann' Stevens: Journalist who claimed to have discovered the Nazi Bormann while on the *Express*. 'Bormann' turned out to be a Bolivian dentist.

Dr Roy Strangelove: Dr Roy Strong, Director of the Victoria and Albert Museum.

Henry Streep-Porter: Henry Porter, *Sunday Times* journalist who wrote up an interview he had conducted with actress Meryl Streep only for it to be revealed that the actress had in fact been a *Mail on Sunday* reporter and he had been the victim of a hoax.

Street of Shame: Fleet Street, after 1950s newspaper vice stories in which 'streets of shame' were always being discovered.

The Sunset Times: The Sunday Times, whose editor Andrew Neil is enthusiastic about the new 'sunrise' technology.

Talbot!: the *Eye* reported that *Now!* magazine's name had been changed to *Talbot!* in a desperate bid to restore confidence after the car company Chrysler had its name changed to Talbot for that reason.

Tarzan: Michael Heseltine (qv *Brilliantine* and *Gingernuts*).

Teeth: Esther Rantzen, TV personality with prominent choppers (qv *Enid Rancid*).

Wishbone Thighs. Anna Ford, TV newscaster.

Tinkerbell: Tim Bell, Thatcher's favourite adman.

Tired and Emotional: Euphemism for drunk, coined by the *Eye*. First used about George Brown (by his press adviser), whose alcoholic excesses were well known but at that time were not spelled out in the press.

Tiresias: Pseudonym for the secret compiler of the crossword – an extremely vulgar and difficult one – known to be 'a distinguished academic churchman'. It was in fact MP Tom Driberg.

Sir Tit and Bum: Larry Lamb, ex-editor of the *Sun* (qv *Sir Larold Lamb*).

President Toadthrush: President Carter.

Toady: Tony Shrimsley, former editor of *Now!*, who pronounced Richard Ingrams and Auberon Waugh to be 'evil men'.

Princess Tom: Princess Michael of Kent, formerly married to Tom Troubridge (qv *Our Val* and *Princess Pushy*).

The Torygraph: the *Daily Telegraph*.

Mike 'Piggy' Townson: Mike Townson, editor of Thames TV's programme *TV Eye*.

Len Trott: left-wing composite based on Richard Neville, *Oz* editor.

Tugboat: Dennis Watts, property man and Berkshire social climber 'who goes from peer to peer'.

Jill Twaddle: Jill Tweedie, *Guardian* women's page writer.

Two Dinners: The lawyer Lord Goodman, whose appetite

led him on several occasions to partake of more than one evening meal.

Ugandan discussions/talking about Uganda/Third World affairs, etc: an *Eye* euphemism for intimate relations which originated at a party given by Neal and Corinna Ascherson. There, a Ugandan government official was said to be upstairs 'talking about Uganda' to a lady journalist when their absence was noted.

Bernard Unleaven: Bernard Levin, Jewish journalist.

The Usurer of the Valleys: Julian Hodge, Welsh financier.

Our Val: according to the *Eye*, the name other royals have given Princess Michael of Kent – Val being short for Valkyrie (qv *Princess Tom* and *Princess Pushy*).

Baillie Vass: Sir Alec Douglas-Home, so called because the *Aberdeen Evening Express* mixed the captions on adjacent photographs of him and a Scottish official of that name.

Charlie Vass: Charles Douglas-Home, features editor of *The Times* in 1970, later editor, who inherited the 'Vass' from his uncle Alec (qv *Baillie Vass*).

Lord 'Spam' Vestey: Lord Vestey, owner of a meat company in Argentina.

Wakey Wakey Jr: Bill Cotton Jr, son of the bandleader and BBC boss.

Whipper Wallace: Anna Wallace, Prince Charles's ex-girlfriend and an enthusiastic hunter.

Alan Watneys: Alan Watkins, a thirsty political commentator for the *Observer*.

The Weasel: Ian Macleod, Tory politician and editor of the *Spectator*.

Martin 'Sweetie' Webster: Martin Webster, homosexual National Front leader.

Jawn Wells: John Wells, *Eye* contributor with upper-class drawl.

Ambrose Weskit/Arnold Wexter: Arnold Wesker, playwright.

Geoffrey Wheatgerm: Geoffrey Wheatcroft, journalist (qv *The Rigid Man*).

Lord Whelks: Lord Matthews, Express Newspapers proprietor and ex-builder whom the *Eye* portrayed as an East End character (qv *Fingers*).

Who he? Ed. This comes from the habit of Harold Ross, first editor of the *New Yorker*, of writing 'Who he/she?' in the margins of contributors' copy.

The Hon. Winkle: Ian Matthews, son of Lord Matthews, alias *Lord Whelks*.

Godfrey Winsome: The late Godfrey Winn, a star newspaper and magazine journalist who specialised in highly sentimental material.

Wislon: Harold Wilson.

Waste Not Wontner: Sir Hugh Wontner, director of the Savoy Hotel.

Perishing Worthless: Peregrine Worsthorne, *Sunday Telegraph* editor.

Lord Wrath: Lord Reith, first BBC chairman.

Woodrow Wyfront: Woodrow Wyatt, journalist, commentator and former Labour politician.

Sid Yobbo: Derek Jameson, East End ex-*Daily Star* editor, as depicted by Ingrams.

Yvonne: Princess Margaret (qv *Royal Midget*).

Victor Zsa Zsa: Victor Zorza, distinguished foreign correspondent.

INDEX